WILLIAM MEADE DAME
PRIVATE FIRST COMPANY OF RICHMOND HOWITZERS
1864

FROM THE RAPIDAN TO RICHMOND

AND

THE SPOTTSYLVANIA CAMPAIGN

A Sketch in Personal Narrative of the
Scenes a Soldier Saw

By

WILLIAM MEADE DAME, D. D.

1920

To
My Comrades of the Army
of Northern Virginia

From the Rapidan
to Richmond and the
Spottsylvania Campaign

William Meade Dame

ESPRIOS DIGITAL PUBLISHING

WILLIAM MEADE DAME, D. D.
RECTOR MEMORIAL PROTESTANT EPISCOPAL CHURCH
BALTIMORE, MD.
1920

INTRODUCTION

By

Thomas Nelson Page

"The land where I was born" was, in my childhood, a great battleground. War—as we then thought the vastest of all wars, not only that had been, but that could ever be—swept over it. I never knew in those days a man who had not been in the war. So, "The War" was the main subject in every discussion and it was discussed with wonderful acumen. Later it took on a different relation to the new life that sprung up and it bore its part in every gathering much as the stories of Troy might have done in the land where Homer sang. To survive, however, in these reunions as a narrator one had to be a real contributor to the knowledge of his hearers. And the first requisite was that he should have been an actor in the scenes he depicted; secondly, that he should know how to depict them. Nothing less served. His hearers themselves all had experience and demanded at least not less than their own. As the time grew more distant they demanded that it should be preserved in more definite form and the details of the life grew more precious.

Among those whom I knew in those days as a delightful narrator of experiences and observations—not of strategy nor even of tactics in battle; but of the life in the midst of the battles in the momentous campaign in which the war was eventually fought out, was a kinsman of mine—the author of this book. A delightful raconteur because he had seen and felt himself what he related, he told his story without conscious art, but with that best kind of art: simplicity. Also with perennial freshness; because he told it from his journals written on the spot.

Thus, it came about that I promised that when he should be ready to publish his reminiscences I would write the introduction for them. My introduction is for a story told from journals and reminiscent of a time in the fierce Sixties when, if passion had free rein, the virtues were strengthened by that strife to contribute so greatly a half century later to rescue the world and make it "safe for Democracy."

It was the war—our Civil War—that over a half century later brought ten million of the American youth to enroll themselves in one day to fight for America. It was the work in "the Wilderness" and in those long campaigns, on both sides, which gave fibre to clear the Belleau Wood. It was the spirit of the armies of Lee and Grant which enabled Pershing's army to sweep through the Argonne.

Rome, March 27, 1919.

WOLSELEY'S TRIBUTE TO LEE

The following tribute to Robert E. Lee was written by Lord Wolseley when commander-in-chief of the armies of Great Britain, an office which he held until succeeded by Lord Roberts.

Lord Wolseley had visited General Lee at his headquarters during the progress of the great American conflict. Some time thereafter Wolseley wrote:

"The fierce light which beats upon the throne is as a rushlight in comparison with the electric glare which our newspapers now focus upon the public man in Lee's position. His character has been subjected to that ordeal, and who can point to a spot upon it? His clear, sound judgment, personal courage, untiring activity, genius for war, absolute devotion to his State, mark him out as a public man, as a patriot to be forever remembered by all Americans. His amiability of disposition, deep sympathy with those in pain or sorrow, his love for children, nice sense of personal honor and generous courtesy, endeared him to all his friends. I shall never forget his sweet, winning smile, nor his clean, honest eyes that seemed to look into your heart while they searched your brain. I have met with many of the great men of my time, but Lee alone impressed me with the feeling that I was in the presence of a man who was cast in a grander mold and made of different and finer metal than all other men. He is stamped upon my memory as being apart and superior to all others in every way, a man with whom none I ever knew and few of whom I have read are worthy to be classed. When all the angry feelings aroused by the secession are buried with those that existed when the American Declaration of Independence was written; when Americans can review the history of their last great war with calm impartiality, I believe all will admit that General Lee towered far above all men on either side in that struggle. I believe he will be regarded not only as the most prominent figure of the Confederacy, but as the greatest American of the nineteenth century, whose statue is well worthy to stand on an equal pedestal with that of Washington and whose memory is equally worthy to be enshrined in the hearts of all his countrymen.

"WOLSELEY."

GENERAL ROBERT E. LEE

CONTENTS

INTRODUCTION

The cause of conflict and the call to arms—Those who answered the call—An army of volunteers—Our great leader—The call comes home—First Company Richmond Howitzers—Back to civil life—Origin of this narrative.

I. SKETCH OF CAMP LIFE THE WINTER BEFORE THE SPOTTSYLVANIA CAMPAIGN

Morton's Ford—Building camp quarters—"Housewarming" on parched corn, persimmons and water—Camp duties—Camp recreations—A special entertainment—Confederate soldier rations—A fresh egg—When fiction became fact—Confederate fashion plates—A surprise attack—Wedding bells and a visit home—The soldiers' profession of faith—The example of Lee, Jackson and Stuart—Spring sprouts and a "tar heel" story.

II. BATTLE OF THE WILDERNESS

"Marse Robert" calls to arms—The spirit of the soldiers of the South—Peace fare and fighting ration—Marse Robert's way of making one equal to three—An infantry battle—Arrival of the First Corps—The love that Lee inspired in the men he led—"Windrows" of Federal dead.

III. BATTLES OF SPOTTSYLVANIA COURT HOUSE

Stuart's four thousand cavalry—Greetings on the field of battle—"Jeb" Stuart assigns "a little job"—Wounding of Robert Fulton Moore—A useful discovery—Barksdale's Mississippi Creeper—Kershaw's South Carolina "rice-birds"—Feeling pulses—Where the fight was hottest—Against heavy odds at "Fort Dodge"—"Sticky" mud and yet more "sticky" men—Gregg's Texans to the front—Breakfastless but "ready for customers"—Parrott's reply to Napoleon's twenty to two—The narrow escape of an entire company—Successive attacks by Federal infantry—Eggleston's heroic death—"Texas will never forget Virginia"—Contrast in losses and the reasons therefore—Why Captain Hunter failed to rally his men—Having "a cannon handy"—Grant's neglect of Federal wounded.

IV. Cold Harbor and the Defense of Richmond

The last march of our Howitzer Captain—The bloodiest fifteen minutes of the war—Federal troops refuse to be slaughtered—Dr. Carter "apologizes for getting shot"—Death of Captain McCarthy—A Summary.

INTRODUCTORY

The Cause of Conflict and the Call to Arms

In 1861 a ringing call came to the manhood of the South. The world knows how the men of the South answered that call. Dropping everything, they came from mountains, valleys and plains—from Maryland to Texas, they eagerly crowded to the front, and stood to arms. What for? What moved them? What was in their minds?

Shallow-minded writers have tried hard to make it appear that slavery was the cause of that war; that the Southern men fought to keep their slaves. They utterly miss the point, or purposely pervert the truth.

In days gone by, the theological schoolmen held hot contention over the question as to the kind of wood the Cross of Calvary was made from. In their zeal over this trivial matter, they lost sight of the great thing that did matter; the mighty transaction, and purpose displayed upon that Cross.

In the causes of that war, slavery was only a detail and an occasion. Back of that lay an immensely greater thing; the defense of their rights—the most sacred cause given men on earth, to maintain at every cost. It is the cause of humanity. Through ages it has been, pre-eminently, the cause of the Anglo-Saxon race, for which countless heroes have died. With those men it was to defend the rights of their States to control their own affairs, without dictation from anybody outside; a right not *given*, but *guaranteed* by the Constitution, which those States accepted, most distinctly, under that condition.

It was for that these men came. This was just what they had in their minds; to uphold that solemnly guaranteed constitutional right, distinctly binding all the parties to that compact. The South pleaded with the other parties to the Constitution to observe their guarantee; when they refused, and talked of force, then the men of the South got their guns and came to see about it.

They were Anglo-Saxons. What could you expect? Their fathers had fought and died on exactly this issue—they could do no less. As their noble fathers, so their noble sons pledged their lives, and their sacred honor to uphold the same great cause—peaceably if they could; forcibly if they must.

Those Who Answered the Call

So the men of the South came together. They came from every rank and calling of life—clergymen, bishops, doctors, lawyers, statesmen, governors of states, judges, editors, merchants, mechanics, farmers. One bishop became a lieutenant general; one clergyman, chief of artillery, Army of Northern Virginia. In one artillery battalion three clergymen were cannoneers at the guns. All the students of one Theological Seminary volunteered, and three fell in battle, and all but one were wounded. They came of every age. I personally know of six men over sixty years who volunteered, and served in the ranks, throughout the war; and in the Army of Northern Virginia, more than ten thousand men were under eighteen years of age, many of them sixteen years.

They came of every social condition of life: some of them were the most prominent men in the professional, social, and political life of their States; owners of great estates, employing many slaves; and thousands of them, horny-handed sons of toil, earning their daily bread by their daily labor, who never owned a slave and never would.

There came men of every degree of intellectual equipment—some of them could hardly read, and per contra, in my battery, at the mock burial of a pet crow, there were delivered an original Greek ode, an original Latin oration, and two brilliant eulogies in English—all in honor of that crow; very high obsequies had that bird.

Men who served as cannoneers of that same battery, in after life came to fill the highest positions of trust and influence—from governors and professors of universities, downward; and one became Speaker of the House of Representatives in the United States Congress. Also, it is to be noted that twenty-one men who served in the ranks of the Confederate Army became Bishops of the Episcopal Church after the war.

Of the men who thus gathered from all the Southern land, the first raised regiments were drawn to Virginia, and there organized into an army whose duty it was to cover Richmond, the Capital of the Confederacy—just one hundred miles from Washington, which would naturally be the center of military activities of the hostile armies.

An Army of Volunteers

The body, thus organized, was composed *entirely of volunteers*. Every man in it was there because he wanted to come as his solemn duty. It was made up of regiments from every State in the South—Maryland, Virginia, North and South Carolina, Georgia, Florida, Alabama, Mississippi, Louisiana, Texas, Arkansas and Tennessee. Each State had its quota, and there were many individual volunteers from Kentucky, Missouri and elsewhere. That army was baptized by a name that was to become immortal in the annals of war—"The Army of Northern Virginia."

What memories cluster around that name! Great soldiers, and military critics of all nations of Christendom, including even the men who fought it, have voiced their opinion of that army, and given it high praise. Many of them, duly considering its spirit, and recorded deeds, and the tremendous odds against which it fought, have claimed for it the highest place on the roll of honor, and in the Hall of Fame, among all the armies of history.

Truly it deserves high place! when you think that after four years of heroic courage, devotion, and endurance, never more than half fed, poorly supplied with clothes, often scant of ammunition, holding the field after every battle, that it fought, till the end, worn out at last, it disbanded at Appomattox, when only eight thousand hungry men remained with arms in their hands, and they, defiant, and fighting still, when the white flags began to pass. They surrendered then only because General Lee said they must, because he would not vainly sacrifice another man; and they wept like broken-hearted children when they heard his orders. They would have fought on till the last man dropped, but General Lee said: "No, you, my men, go home and serve your country in peace as you have done in war."

Our Great Leader

They did as General Lee told them to do, and it was the indomitable courage of those men and of the women of their land, who were just as brave, at home, as the men were, at the front, which has made the South rise from its ruins and blossom as the rose as it does this day.

Thus "yielding to overwhelming numbers and resources," the Army of Northern Virginia died. But its *glory* has not died, and the splendor of its deeds has not, and will not grow dim.

As, in vision, I look across the long years that have pressed their length between the now and then, I can see that Army of Northern Virginia on the march. At its head rides one august and knightly figure, Robert E. Lee, the knightliest gentleman, and the saintliest hero that our race has bred. He is on old "Traveler," almost as famous as his master. On his right rides that thunderbolt of war, Stonewall Jackson, on "Little Sorrel," with whose fame the world was ringing when he fell. On Lee's left, on his beautiful mare, "Lady Annie," the bright, flashing cavalier, "Jeb" Stuart, the darling of the Army.

Behind these three, in their swinging stride, tramp the long columns of infantry, artillery, and cavalry of the army. As we gaze upon that spectacle, we say, and nothing better can be said, "Those chiefs were worthy to lead those soldiers; those soldiers were worthy to follow Robert Lee."

In this order, The Army of Northern Virginia, General Lee in front, has come marching down the road of history, and shall march on, and all brave souls of the generations stand at "Salute," and do them homage as they pass. Noble Army of Northern Virginia!

All true men will understand and none, least of all the brave men who faced it in battle, will deny to the old Confederate the just right to be proud that he was comrade to those men and marched in their ranks, and was with their leader to the end. Of that army, I had, thank God! the honor to be a soldier. It came about in this way.

The Call Comes Home

When the war began I was a school boy attending the Military Academy in Danville, Virginia, where I was born and reared. At once the school broke up. The teachers, and all the boys who were old enough went into the army. I was just sixteen years old, and small for my age, and I can understand now, but could not then, how my parents looked upon the desire of a boy like that to go to the war, as out of the question. I did not think so. I was a strong, well-knit fellow, and it seemed to me that what you required in a soldier was a man who could shoot, and would stay there and do it. I knew I could shoot, and I thought I could stay there and do it, so I was sure I could be a soldier, and I was crazy to go, but my parents could not see it so, and I was very miserable. All my classmates in school had gone or were going, and I pictured to myself the boys coming back from the war, as soldiers who had been in battle, and all the honors that would be showered upon them—and I would be out of it all. The thought that I had not done a manly part in this great crisis would make me feel disgraced all my life. It was horrible.

My father, the honored and beloved minister of the Episcopal Church in Danville, and my mother, the daughter and granddaughter of two Revolutionary soldiers, said they wanted me to go, and would let me go, when I was older—I was too young and small as yet. But I was afraid it would be all over before I got in, and I would lay awake at night, sad and wretched with this fear. I need not have been afraid of that. There was going to be plenty to go around, but I did not know that then, and I was low in mind. I suppose that my very strong feeling on the subject was natural. It was the inherited microbe in the blood. Though I was only a school boy in a back country town, my forebears had always been around when there was any fighting to be done. My great-grandfather, General Thomas Nelson, and my grandfather, Major Carter Page, and all their kin of the time had fought through the Revolutionary War. My people had fought in the war of 1812, and the Mexican War, and the Indian Wars. Whenever anybody was fighting our country, some of my people were in it, and back of that, Lord Nelson of Trafalgar, was a second cousin of my great-grandfather, Thomas Nelson; and, still farther back of that, my ancestor, Thomas Randolph, in command of a division of the Scottish Army under King Robert Bruce, was the man who, by his furious charge, broke the English line at "Bannockburn" and won the Independence of Scotland.

You see that a boy, with all that back of him, in his family, had the virus in his blood, and could not help being wretched when his country was invaded, and fighting, and he not in it. He would feel that he was dishonoring the traditions of his race, and untrue to the memory of his fathers. However, that schoolboy brooding over the situation was mighty miserable. When my parents realized my feelings, they, at last, gave up their opposition, and I went into the army with their consent, and blessing.

First Company Richmond Howitzers

While this matter was hanging fire, having been at a military academy, I was trying to do some little service by helping to drill some of the raw companies which were being rapidly raised, in and around Danville. The minute I was free, off I went. Circumstances led me to enlist in a battery made up in Richmond, known as the

"First Company of Richmond Howitzers," and I was thus associated with as fine a body of men as ever lived—who were to be my comrades in arms, and the most loved, and valued friends of my after life.

This battery was attached to "Cabell's Battalion" and formed part of the field artillery of Longstreet's Corps, Army of Northern Virginia. It was a "crack" battery, and was always put in when anything was going on. It served with great credit, and was several times mentioned in General Orders, as having rendered signal service to the army. It was in all the campaigns, and in action in every battle of the Army of Northern Virginia. It fought at Manassas, Williamsburg, Seven Pines, Seven Days' Battle around Richmond in 1862, Second Manassas, Sharpsburg, Harpers Ferry, Fredericksburg, Chancellorsville, Gettysburg, Morton's Ford, The Wilderness, The Battles of Spottsylvania Court House, North Anna, Pole Green Church, Cold Harbor, Petersburg, and at Appomattox Court House. Every one of the cannoneers, who had not been killed or wounded, was at his gun in its last fight. The very last thing it did was to help "wipe up the ground" with some of Sheridan's Cavalry, which attacked and tried to ride us down, but was cut to pieces by our cannister fire, and went off as hard as their horses could run—as if the devil was after them. Then the surrender closed our service.

Back to Civil Life

My comrades, as the rest of the army, scattered to their homes. I went to my home in Danville, and had to walk 180 miles to get there. After a few days, which I chiefly employed in trying to get rid of the sensation of starving, I went to work—got a place in the railroad service.

After eighteen months of this, I proceeded to carry out a purpose that I had in mind since the closing days of the war. I had been through that long and bloody conflict; I had been at my gun every time it went into action, except once when I was lying ill of typhoid fever; I had been in the path of death many times, and though hit several times, had never been seriously wounded, or hurt badly enough to have to leave my gun—and here I was at the end of all this—alive, and well and strong, and twenty years of age. As I thought of God's merciful protection through all those years of hardship and danger, a wish and purpose was born, and got fixed in my mind and heart, to devote my life to the service of God in the completest way I could as a thanksgiving to Him. Naturally, my thoughts turned to the ministry of the Gospel, and I decided to enter the seminary and train for that service as soon as the way was open.

While I was in the railroad train work, I studied hard in the scraps of time to get some preparation, and in September, 1866, I entered the Virginia Theological Seminary along with twenty-five other students—all of whom were Confederate soldiers. I here tackled a job that was much more trying than working my old twelve-pounder brass Napoleon gun in a fight. I would willingly have swapped jobs, if it had been all the same, but I worked away, the best I could, at the Hebrew, and Greek, and "Theology," and all the rest, for three years.

Somehow I got through, and graduated, and was ordained by Bishop Johns of Virginia, the twenty-sixth of June, 1869. Thus the old cannoneer was transformed into a parson, who intended to try to be as faithful to duty, as a parson, as the old cannoneer had been. He has carried that purpose through life ever since. How far he has realized it, others will have to judge.

After serving for nine years in several parishes in Virginia, I came to Baltimore as rector of Memorial Church, and have been here ever since. Hence I have served in the ministry for fifty years—forty-one of which I have spent serving the Memorial Church, and having, as a side line, been Chaplain of the "Fifth Regiment Maryland National Guard" for thirty-odd years. When one is bitten by the military "bee" in his youth, he never gets over it—the sight of a line of soldiers, and the sound of martial music stirs me still, as it always did, and I have had the keenest interest and pleasure in my association with that splendid regiment, and my dear friends and comrades in it.

So, through the changes and chances of this mortal life, I have come thus far, and by the blessing of God, and the patience of my people, at the age of seventy-four I am still in full work among the people, whom I have served so long, and loved so well—still at my post where I hope to stay till the Great Captain orders me off to service in the only place I know of, that is better than the congregation of Memorial Church, and the community of Baltimore—and that is the everlasting Kingdom of Heaven.

Origin of This Narrative

Now, what I have been writing here is intended to lead up to the narrative set forth in the pages of this volume. Sam Weller once said to Mr. Pickwick, when invited to eat a veal pie, "Weal pies is werry good, providin' you knows the lady as makes 'em, and is sure that they *is weal* and not *cats*." The remark applies here: a narrative is "werry good providin' you knows" the man as makes it, and are sure that it is facts, and not fancy tales. You want to be satisfied that the writer was a personal witness of the things he writes about, and is one who can be trusted to tell you things as he actually saw them. I hope both these conditions are fulfilled in this narrative.

But some one might say, "How about this narrative that you are about to impose on a suffering public, who never did you any harm? What do you do it for?"

Well, I did not do it of malice aforethought. It came about in this way. Young as I was when I went into the war, and never having seen anything of the world outside the ordinary life of a boy, in a quiet country town, the scenes of that soldier life made a deep impression on my mind, and I have carried a very clear recollection of them—everyone—in my memory ever since. As I have looked back, and thought upon the events, and especially the spirit, and character, and record, of my old comrades in that army, my admiration, and estimate of their high worth as soldiers has grown ever greater, and I felt a very natural desire that others should know them as I knew them—and put them in their rightful rank as soldiers. The only way to do this is for those who know to tell people about them; what manner of warriors they were.

Now mark how one glides into mischief unintentionally. Years ago, I was beguiled into making, at various times, places, and occasions, certain, what might be called, "Camp Fire Talks" descriptive of Soldier Life in the Army of Northern Virginia. Weakly led on by the kindly expressed opinions of those who heard these talks, and urged by old friends, and comrades, and others, I ventured on a more connected narrative of our observations and experiences, as soldiers in that army. I wrote a sketch, in that vein, of the "Spottsylvania Campaign"—in 1864—fought between General Lee and General Grant. It was a tremendous struggle of the two armies for thirty days—almost without a break. It was a thrilling period of the war, and brought out the high quality of both the Commander and the fighting men of the Army of Northern Virginia.

It was the bloodiest struggle known to history, up to that time. As one item, at Cold Harbor, General Grant, in fifteen minutes, by the watch, lost 13,723 men, killed and wounded, irrespective of many prisoners—more men in a quarter of an hour than the British Army lost in the whole battle of Waterloo. That gives an idea of the terrible intensity of that campaign—one incident of it the bloodiest quarter of an hour in all the history of war.

I took as a title for my sketch "From the Rapidan to Richmond" or "The Bloody War Path of 1864"—"The Scenes One Soldier Saw."

As a guarantee of its accuracy, I took that narrative to Richmond, and in the presence of fifteen of my old comrades of the First Howitzers, every man of whom had been along with me through all the incidents of which I wrote, and therefore had personal knowledge of all the facts, I read it, and we freely discussed it. What resulted has the approval, and endorsement of all those personal witnesses, and may be counted on as accurate—in every statement and impression made in this story, and may be safely accepted by the reader as a true narration of facts.

I am urged to put the narrative in such form that its contents may be more widely known, and I am glad to do it. I do want as many as possible to know my old comrades as I knew them, and value them at their true worth. My narrative is a true account of that soldier life, and illustrates the stuff of which those men of the Army of Northern Virginia were made. The story illustrates this in a graphic and impressive way, because it is a simple and homely story of how they lived, and what they did—showing what they were. It is an honorable testimony to the character, and worth, as patriot soldiers, of my old comrades—borne by one who saw them display their courage, and endurance, and devotion in heroic conduct, in every possible way, through the long strain, and stress of war—to the end.

I believe there is interest and value, to the true understanding of history, in such narratives of personal witnesses to the men, and things, and conditions of that past, which reflected so much glory on the manhood of our American race; which sterling quality, of high soldierly worth, has just been shown again, in the present generation of our race, when American soldiers, drawn from the North, South, East and West have stood, shoulder to shoulder, in the one American line, under the Star-Spangled Banner, and fighting for the freedom of the world. Our splendid American men of today are what they are, and have done what they did, because the blood of their sires runs in them; because they are "the same breed of dogs" with the American soldiers, who, on both sides, in the bloody struggle of the Civil War, bore them so bravely in the days gone by.

This narrative only paints the picture, and gives a sample of the Anglo-Saxon American soldier of the generation just gone; it shed lustre upon our race. This generation has done the same—all honor to both!

A Summary

Let us Americans, at all cost, keep pure the Anglo-Saxon blood, to which this America belongs, of right; let us as a nation, Americans all, work and dwell together in true comradeship, and let our nation walk in just and right ways, for our country. Then, indeed, our heart's aspiration shall be fulfilled.

> "And the Star-Spangled Banner *forever* shall wave
> O'er the land of the free—and the home of the brave."

As a preface to the sketch of the active campaign, I have given some account of our life in the winter quarters camp, the winter before, from which we marched to battle when the Spottsylvania Campaign opened.

CHAPTER I

SKETCH OF CAMP LIFE THE WINTER BEFORE THE SPOTTSYLVANIA CAMPAIGN

Morton's Ford

From Orange Court House, Virginia, the road running northeast into Culpeper crosses Morton's Ford of the Rapidan River, which, in December, 1863, lay between the "Federal Army of the Potomac" and the "Confederate Army of Northern Virginia." The Ford is nineteen miles from Orange Court House.

Just after the battle of Mine Run, November 26 to 28, our Battery left its bivouac near the Court House, and marched to the Ford. As the road reaches a point within three-quarters of a mile of the river, it rises over a sharp hill and thence winds its way down the hill to the Ford. On the ridge, just where the road crosses it, the guns of the Battery, First Company of Richmond Howitzers, were placed in position, commanding the Ford, and the Howitzer Camp was to the right of the road, in the pine woods just back of the ridge. We had been sent here to help the Infantry pickets to watch the enemy, and guard the Ford. Orders were that we should remain in this position all winter, and were to make ourselves as comfortable as we could, with a view to this long stay. We got there December 2 and 3, and, in fact, did stay there until the opening of the spring campaign, May 3, 1864.

Building Camp Quarters

With these instructions, as soon as we placed our guns in battery on the hill, we went promptly to work to fix up winter quarters in the shelter of the pines down the hill just a few rods back of the guns. It was getting very cold, and rough weather threatened, so we pitched in and worked hard to get ready for it.

Each group of tent mates chose their own site and thereon built such a house as suited their energy, and judgment, or fancy. Some few of the lazy ones stayed under canvas all winter, but most of us constructed better quarters. In my group, four of us lived together, and we built after this manner. On our selected site, we marked off a space about ten feet square. We dug to the line all around, and to a depth of three or four feet in the ground—this going below the surface of the ground gave a better protection against wind and cold than any wall one could build—and on that bleak hill you wanted all the shield from wind that you could get. Having dug a hole ten feet square and three feet deep, we went into the woods and cut, squared, and carried on our shoulders logs, twelve or eighteen inches thick, and twelve feet long—enough to build around three sides of that hole a wall four feet high. Half of the fourth side was taken up by the chimney, which was built of short logs split in half and covered well inside with mud. With such suitable stones as we could pick up, we lined the fire place immediately around the fire, and as far above as we had rocks to do it with. The other half of the fourth side was left for the door, over which was hung any old blanket or other cloth that we could beg, borrow or steal.

The log walls done, we dug a deep hole, loosened up the clay at the bottom, poured in water and mixed up a lot of mud with which we chinked up the interstices between the logs and covered the wood in the chimney. The earth that had been thrown up in digging the hole, we now banked up against the log wall all around, which made it wind proof; and then over this gem of architecture we stretched our fly. We had no closed tents—only a fly, a straight piece of tent cloth all open at the sides. Our fly, supported by a rude pole, and drawn down and firmly fastened to the top of the log wall, made the roof of the house.

"Housewarming" on Parched Corn, Persimmons and Water

Then we went out and cut small poles and made a bunk, to lift us off the ground. Over the expanse of springy poles we spread sprigs of cedar—and this made a pretty good spring mattress. Last of all, we dug a ditch all around our house to keep the water from draining down into our room and driving us out. Then we went in, built a fire in our fireplace, called in our friends, and had a house-warming. The refreshments were parched corn, persimmons (which two of us walked two miles to get) and water. Of the latter, we had plenty in canteens borrowed from the boys. We had a bully time, and we kept it up late. Then we went to bed in our cosy bunk and slept like graven images till reveille next morning. Thus we were housed for the winter—"under our own vine and fig tree," so to speak.

Most of the other houses were built after the same general style. We bragged that we had the best house in camp, and were very chesty about it. Others did likewise.

The men's quarters ready, we at once set to work on stables for the horses, of which there were about seventy, belonging to the Battery. All hands were called in to do this work. We scattered through the woods, cut logs and carried them on our shoulders to the spot selected. We built up walls around three sides, leaving the fourth or sunny side open. Then we cut logs into three or four foot lengths and split them into slabs, and with these slabs, as a rough sort of shingle, covered the roof and weighted them down, in place, with long, heavy logs laid across each row of slabs. Then we mixed mud and stopped up the cracks in the log walls. Altogether, we had a good, strong wind and rain-proof building, which was an effective shelter for the horses and in which they kept dry and comfortable through the winter—which was a cold and stormy one. All the men worked hard, and we soon had the stable finished, and the horses housed. Thus our building work was done, and we settled into the regular routine of camp life.

Camp Duties

Perhaps a little sketch of our life in winter quarters, how we lived, how we employed ourselves, and what we did to pass away the time, may be interesting. I will try to give you some account of all that.

Of course, we all had our military duties to attend to regularly. The drivers had to clean, feed, water, and exercise the horses, and keep the stables in order. The "cannoneers" had to keep the guns clean, bright, and ready for service any minute—also they had to stand guard at the guns on the hill all the time, and over the camp, at night, to guard the forage, and look after things generally. We had to drill some every day—police the camp and keep the roads near the camp in order. To this day's work we were called, every morning at six o'clock, by the bugler blowing the reveille. I may mention the fact that Prof. Francis Nicholas Crouch, the composer of the famous and beautiful song, "Kathleen Mavourneen," was the bugler of our Battery, and he was the heartless wretch who used to persecute us that way. To be waked up and hauled out about day dawn on a cold, wet, dismal morning, and to have to hustle out and stand shivering at roll call, was about the most exasperating item of the soldier's life. The boys had a song very expressive of a soldier's feelings when nestling in his warm blankets, he heard the malicious bray of that bugle. It went like this:

From the Rapidan to Richmond and the Spottsylvania Campaign

"Oh, how I hate to get up in the morning;
  Oh, how I'd like to remain in bed.
But the saddest blow of all is to hear the bugler call,
  'You've got to get up, you've got to get up,
You've got to get up this morning!'

"Some day I'm going to murder that bugler;
  Some day they're going to find him dead.
I'll amputate his reveille,
And stamp upon it heavily,
  And spend the rest of my life in bed!"

We didn't kill old Crouch—I don't know why, except that he was protected by a special providence, which sometimes permits such evil deeds to go unpunished. We used to hope that he would blow his own brains out, through his bugle, but he didn't—he lived many years after the war.

Camp Recreations

In between our stated duties, we had some time in which we could amuse ourselves as we chose, and we had many means of entertainment. We had a chessboard and men—a set of quoits, dominoes, and cards; and there was the highly intellectual game of "push pin" open to all comers. Some very skillful chess players were discovered in the company. When the weather served, we had games of ball, and other athletic games, such as foot races, jumping, boxing, wrestling, lifting heavy weights, etc. At night we would gather in congenial groups around the camp fires and talk and smoke and "swap lies," as the boys expressed it.

There was one thing from which we got a great deal of fun. We got up an organization amongst the youngsters which was called the "Independent Battalion of Fusiliers." The basal principle of this kind of heroes was, "In an advance, always in the rear—in a retreat, always in front. Never do anything that you can help. The chief aim of life is to rest. If you should get to a gate, don't go to the exertion of opening it. Sit down and wait until somebody comes along and opens it for you."

After the first organizers, no one applied for admission into the Battalion—they were elected into it, without their consent. The way we kept the ranks full was this: Whenever any man in the Battery did any specially trifling, and good-for-nothing thing, or was guilty of any particularly asinine conduct, or did any fool trick, or expressed any idiotic opinion, he was marked out as a desirable recruit for the Fusiliers. We elected him, went and got him and made him march with us in parade of the Battalion, and solemnly invested him with the honor. This was not always a peaceable performance. Sometimes the candidate, not appreciating his privilege, had to be held by force, and was struggling violently, and saying many bad words, during the address of welcome by the C. O.

I grieve to say that an election into this notable corps was treated as an insult, and responded to by hot and unbecoming language. One fellow, when informed of his election, flew into a rage, and said bad words, and offered to lick the whole Battalion. But what would they have? We were obliged to fill up the ranks.

After a while it did come to be better understood, and was treated as a joke, and some of the more sober men entered into the fun, and would go out on parade, and take part in the ceremony. We paraded with a band composed of men beating tin buckets, frying pans, and canteens, with sticks, and whistling military music. It made a noisy and impressive procession. It attracted much attention and furnished much amusement to the camp.

A Special Entertainment

On proper occasions, promotions to higher rank were made for distinguished merit in our line. An instance will illustrate. One night, late, I was passing along when I saw this sight. The sentinel on guard in camp was lying down on a pile of bags of corn at the forage pile — sound asleep. He was lying on his left side. One of the long tails of his coat was hanging loose from his body and dangling down alongside the pile of bags. A half-grown cow had noiselessly sneaked up to the forage pile, and been attracted by that piece of cloth hanging loose—and, as calves will do, took the end of it into her mouth and was chewing it with great satisfaction. I called several of the fellows, and we watched the proceedings. The calf got more and more of the coat tail into her mouth. At length, with her mouth full of the cloth, and perhaps with the purpose of swallowing what she had been chewing she gave a hard jerk. The cloth was old, the seams rotten—that jerk pulled the whole of that tail loose from the body of the coat. The sleeping guard never moved. We rescued the cloth from the calf, and hid it. When the sleeper awoke, to his surprise, one whole tail of his coat was gone, and he was left with only one of the long tails. Our watching group, highly delighted at the show of a sentinel sleeping, while a calf was browsing on him, told him what had happened and that the calf had carried off the other coat tail. He was inconsolable. He was the only private in the company who had a long-tailed coat and it was the pride of his heart. There was no way of repairing the loss, and he had to go around for days, sad and dejected, shorn of his glory—with only one tail to his coat.

All this was represented to the "Battalion of Fusiliers." Charges were preferred, and the Court Martial set. The witnesses testified to the facts—also said that if we had not driven off the calf it would have gone on, after getting the coat tail, and chewed up the sentinel, too. The findings of the Court Martial were nicely adjusted to the merits of the case. It was, that the witnesses were sentenced to punishment for driving off the calf, and not letting her eat up the sentinel.

For the sentinel, who appeared before the Court with the one tail to his coat, it was decreed that his conduct was the very limit. No one could ever hope to find a more thorough Fusilier than the man who went to sleep on guard and let a calf eat his clothes off. Such conduct deserved most distinguished regard, as an encouragement to the Fusiliers. He was promoted to the rank of Lieutenant-General of the Battalion, the highest rank in our corps. After a while the lost coat tail was produced, and sewed on again.

Confederate Soldier Rations

The one thing that we suffered most from, the hardship hardest to bear, was hunger. The scantiness of the rations was something fierce. We never got a square meal that winter. We were always hungry. Even when we were getting full rations the issue was one-quarter pound of bacon, or one-half pound of beef, and little over a pint of flour or cornmeal, ground with the cob on it, we used to think—no stated ration of vegetables or sugar and coffee—just bread and meat. Some days we had the bread, but no meat; some days the meat, but no bread. Two days we had nothing, neither bread nor meat—and it was a solemn and empty crowd. Now and then, at long intervals, they gave us some dried peas. Occasionally, a little sugar—about an ounce to a man for a three days' ration. The Orderly of the mess would spread the whole amount on the back of a tin plate, and mark off thirteen portions, and put each man's share into his hand—three days' rations, this was. One time, in a burst of generosity, the Commissary Department stunned us by issuing coffee. We made "coffee" out of most anything—parched corn, wheat or rye—when we could get it. Anything for a hot drink at breakfast! But this was *coffee*—"sure enough" coffee—we called it. They issued this three times. The first time, when counted out to the consumer, by the Orderly, each man had 27 grains. He made a cup—drank it. The next time the issue was 16 grains to the man—again he made a cup and drank it. The third issue gave nine grains to the man. Each of these issues was for three days' rations. By now it had got down to being a joke, so we agreed to put the whole amount together, and draw for which one of the mess should have it all—with the condition, that the winner should make a pot of coffee, and drink it, and let the rest of us see him do it. This was done. Ben Lambert won—made the pot of coffee—sat on the ground, with us twelve, like a coroner's jury, sitting around watching him, and drank every drop. How he could do it, under the gaze of twelve hungry men, who had no coffee, it is hard to see, but Ben was capable of very difficult feats. He drank that pot of coffee—all the same!

After this, there was no more issue of coffee. Even a Commissary began to be dimly conscious that nine grains given a man for a three days' rations was like joking with a serious subject, so they quit it, and during that winter we had mostly just bread and meat—very little of that, and that little not to be counted on.

This hunger was much the hardest trial we had to bear. We didn't much mind getting wet and cold; working hard, standing guard at night; and fighting when required—we were seasoned to all that— but you don't season to hunger. Going along all day with a gnawing at your insides, of which you were always conscious, was not pleasant. We had more appetite than anything else, and never got enough to satisfy it—even for a time.

Under this very strict regime, eating was like to become a lost art and our digestive organs had very little to do. We had very little use for them, in these days. A story went around the camp to this effect: One of the men got sick—said he had a pain in his stomach and sent for the surgeon. The doctor, trying to find the trouble, felt the patient's abdomen, and punched it, here and there. After a while he felt a hard lump, which ought not to be there. The doctor wondered what it could be—then feeling about, he found another hard lump, and then another, and another. Then the doctor was perfectly mystified by all those hard places in a man's insides. At last, the explanation came to him: he was feeling the vertebræ of the fellow's back-bone— right through his stomach!

I do not vouch for the exact accuracy of all the details of the story, but it illustrates the situation. We all felt that our stomachs had dwindled away for want of use and exercise.

A Fresh Egg

Another incident, that I can vouch for, showing the strenuous time the whole army had about food that winter: One day Major-Quartermaster John Ludlow, of Norfolk, met a Captain of Artillery from his own town of Norfolk—Capt. Charles Grandy, of the Norfolk Light Artillery Blues. The Major invited the Captain to dine with him on a certain day. He did not expect anything very much, but there was a seductive sound in the word "dining" and he accepted. Grandy told the story of his experience on that festive occasion. He walked two miles to Major Ludlow's quarters, and was met with friendly cordiality by his old fellow-townsman, and ushered into his hut where a bright fire was burning. After a time spent in conversation, the Major began to prepare for dinner. He reached up on a shelf, and took down a cake of bread, cut it into two pieces, and put them in a frying pan on the fire to heat. Then he reached up on the shelf and got down a piece of bacon—not very large—cut it into two pieces, and put them in another pan on the fire to fry. Down in the ashes by the fire was a tin cup covered over—its contents not visible. The dining table was an old door, taken from some barn and set up on skids.

When the bread and meat were ready, the Major put it on the table and with a courtly wave of his hand said, "D-d-draw up, Charley." They seated themselves. The Major gave a piece of bread and a piece of bacon to his guest, and took the other piece, of each, for himself. After he had eaten a while—the Major got up, went to the fireplace and took up the tin cup. He poured off the water, and, behold, one egg came to view. This egg, the Major put on a plate and, coming to the table, handed it to Grandy—"Ch-Ch-Charley, take an egg," as if there were a dish full. Charley, having been brought up to think it not good manners to take the last thing on the dish, declined to take the only egg in sight—said he didn't care specially for eggs! though he said he would have given a heap for that egg, as he hadn't tasted one since he had been in the army. "But," urged the Major, "Ch-Ch-Charley, I insist that you take an egg. You must take one—there is going to be plenty—do take it." Under this encouragement, Grandy took the egg—while he was greatly enjoying it, suddenly there was a flutter in the corner of the hut. An old hen flew up from behind a box in the corner, lit on the side of the box and began to cackle loudly.

The Major turned to Grandy and said, "I-I t-t-told you there was going to be a plenty. I invited you to dinner today because this was the day for the hen to lay." He went over and got the fresh egg from behind the box, cooked and ate it. So each of the diners had an egg. The incident was suggestive of the situation. Here was a Quartermaster appointing a day for dining a friend—depending for part of the feast on his confidence that his hen would come to time. The picture of that formal dinner in the winter quarters on the Rapidan is worth drawing. It was a fair sign of the times, and of life in the Army of Northern Virginia; when it came to a Quartermaster giving to an honored, and specially invited guest, a dinner like that—it indicates a general scarceness.

When Fiction Became Fact

One bright spot in that "winter of our discontent"—lives in my memory. It was on the Christmas Day of 1863. That was a day specially hard to get through. The rations were very short indeed that day—only a little bread, no meat. As we went, so hungry, about our work, and remembered the good and abundant cheer always belonging to Christmas time; as we thought of "joys we had tasted in past years" that did *not* "return" to us, now, and felt the woeful difference in our insides—it made us sad. It was harder to starve on Christmas Day than any day of the winter.

When the long day was over and night had come, some twelve or fifteen of us, congenial comrades, had gathered in a group, and were sitting out of doors around a big camp fire, talking about Christmas, and trying to keep warm and cheer ourselves up.

One fellow proposed what he called a *game*, and it was at once taken up—though it was a silly thing to do, as it only made us hungrier than ever. The game was this—we were to work our fancy, and imagine that we were around the table at "Pizzini's," in Richmond. Pizzini was the famous restauranteur who was able to keep up a wonderful eating house all through the war, even when the rest of Richmond was nearly starving. Well—in reality, now, we were all seated on the ground around that fire, and very hungry. In imagination we were all gathered 'round Pizzini's with unlimited credit and free to call for just what we wished. One fellow tied a towel on him, and acted as the waiter—with pencil and paper in hand going from guest to guest taking orders—all with the utmost gravity. "Well, sir, what will you have?" he said to the first man. He thought for a moment and then said (I recall that first order, it was monumental) "I will have, let me see—a four-pound steak, a turkey, a jowl and turnip tops, a peck of potatoes, six dozen biscuits, plenty of butter, a large pot of coffee, a gallon of milk and six pies—three lemon and three mince—and hurry up, waiter—that will do for a start; see 'bout the rest later."

This was an order for one, mind you. The next several were like unto it. Then, one guest said, "I will take a large saddle of mountain mutton, with a gallon of crabapple jelly to eat with it, and as much as you can tote of other things."

This, specially the crabapple jelly, quite struck the next man. He said, "I will take just the same as this gentleman." So the next, and the next. All the rest of the guests took the mountain mutton and jelly.

All this absurd performance was gone through with all seriousness—making us wild with suggestions of good things to eat and plenty of it.

The waiter took all the orders and carefully wrote them down, and read them out to the guest to be sure he had them right.

Just as we were nearly through with this Barmecide feast, one of the boys, coming past us from the Commissary tent, called out to me, "Billy, old Tuck is just in (Tucker drove the Commissary wagon and went up to Orange for rations) and I think there is a box, or something, for you down at the tent."

I got one of our crowd to go with me on the jump. Sure enough, there was a great big box for me—from home. We got it on our shoulders and trotted back up to the fire. The fellows gathered around, the top was off that box in a jiffy, and there, right on top, the first thing we came to—funny to tell, after what had just occurred— was the biggest saddle of mountain mutton, and a two-gallon jar of crabapple jelly to eat with it. The box was packed with all good, solid things to eat—about a bushel of biscuits and butter and sausage and pies, etc., etc.

We all pitched in with a whoop. In ten minutes after the top was off, there was not a thing left in that box except one skin of sausage which I saved for our mess next morning. You can imagine how the boys did enjoy it. It was a bully way to end up that hungry Christmas Day.

From the Rapidan to Richmond and the Spottsylvania Campaign

I wrote my thanks and the thanks of all the boys to my mother and sisters, who had packed that box, and I described the scene as I have here described it, which made them realize how welcome and acceptable their kind present was—and what comfort and pleasure it gave—all the more that it came to us on Christmas Day, and made it a joyful one—at the end, at least.

In regard to all this low diet from which we suffered so much hunger that winter—it is well worthy of remark that the health of the army was never better. At one time that winter there were only 300 men in hospital from the whole Army of Northern Virginia—which seems to suggest that humans don't need as much to eat as they think they do. That army was very hungry, but it was very healthy! It looks like cause and effect! But it was a very painful way of keeping healthy. I fear we would not have taken that tonic, if we could have helped it, but we couldn't! Maybe it was best as it was. Let us hope so!

Well, the winter wore on in this regular way until the 3d or 4th of February, when our quiet was suddenly disturbed in a most unexpected manner. Right in the dead of a stormy winter, when nobody looked for any military move—we had a fight. The enemy got "funny" and we had to bring him to a more serious state of mind, and teach him how wrong it was to disturb the repose of gentlemen when they were not looking for it, and not doing anything to anybody—just trying to be happy, and peaceable if they could get a chance.

Confederate Fashion Plates

Leading up to an account of this, I may mention some circumstances in the way of the boys in the camp. Living the hard life, we were—one would suppose that fashion was not in all our thoughts; but even then, we felt the call of fashion and followed it in such lines, as were open to us. The instinct to "do as the other fellow does" is implanted in humans by nature; this blind impulse explains many things that otherwise were inexplicable. With the ladies it makes many of them wear hats and dresses that make them look like hoboes and guys, and shoes that make them walk about as gracefully as a cow in a blanket, instead of looking, and moving like the young, graceful gazelles—that nature meant, and men want them to look like. Taste and grace and modesty go for nothing—when fashion calls.

Well, the blind impulse that affects the ladies so—moved us in regard to the patches put on the seats of our pants. This was the only particular in which we could depart from the monotony of our quiet, simple, gray uniform—which consisted of a jacket, and pants and did not lend itself to much variety; but fashion found a way.

There must always be a leader of fashion. We had one—"The glass of fashion and the mould of form" in our gang was Ben Lambert. He could look like a tombstone, but was full of fun, and inventive genius.

Our uniform was a short jacket coming down only to the waist, hence a hole in the seat of the pants was conspicuous, and was regarded as not suited to the dignity and soldierly appearance of a Howitzer. For one to go around with such a hole showing—any longer than he could help it—was considered a want of respect to his comrades. Public opinion demanded that these holes be stopped up as soon as possible. Sitting about on rough surfaces—as stumps, logs, rocks, and the ground—made many breaks in the integrity of pants, and caused need of frequent repairs, for ours was not as those of the ancient Hebrews to whom Moses said, "Thy raiment waxed not old upon thee"—ours waxed very old, before we could get another pair, and were easily rubbed through. The more sedate men were content with a plain, unpretentious patch, but this did not satisfy the youngsters, whose æsthetic souls yearned for "they know not what," until Ben Lambert showed them. One morning he appeared at roll call with a large patch in the shape of a heart transfixed with an arrow, done out of red flannel. This at once won the admiration and envy of the soldiers. They now saw what they wished, in the way of a patch, and proceeded to get it. Each one set his ingenuity to work to devise something unique. Soon the results began to appear. Upon the seats of one, and another, and another, were displayed figures of birds, beasts and men—a spread eagle, a cow, a horse, a cannon. One artist depicted a "Cupid" with his bow, and just across on the other hip a heart pierced with an arrow from Cupid's bow—all wrought out of red flannel and sewed on as patches to cover the holes in the pants, and, at the same time, present a pleasing appearance. By and by these devices increased in number, and when the company was fallen in for roll call the line, seen from the rear, presented a very gay and festive effect.

One morning, a General, who happened in camp—the gallant soldier, and merry Irishman, General Pat Finnegan, was standing, with our Captain, in front of the line, hearing the roll call.

That done, the Orderly Sergeant gave the order, "'Bout face!" The rear of the line was thus turned toward General Finnegan. When that art gallery—in red flannel—was suddenly displayed to his delighted eyes the General nearly laughed himself into a fit.

"Oh, boys," he cried out, "don't ever turn your backs upon the enemy. Sure they'll git ye—red makes a divil of a good target. But I wouldn't have missed this for the world."

The effect, as seen from the rear, was impressive. It could have been seen a mile off—bright red patches on dull gray cloth. Anyhow it was better than the holes and it made a ruddy glow in camp. Also it gave the men much to amuse them.

Ben set the fashion in one other particular—viz., in hair cuts. He would come to roll call with his hair cut in some peculiar way, and stand in rank perfectly solemn. Ranks broken, the boys would gather eagerly about him, and he would announce the name of that "cut." They would, as soon as they could, get their hair cut in the same style.

One morning, he stood in rank with every particle of his hair cut off, as if shaved, and his head as bare as a door knob. "What style is that, Ben?" the boys asked. "The 'horse thief' cut," he gravely announced. Their one ambition now, was to acquire the "horse-thief cut."

There was only one man in the Battery who could cut hair—Sergeant Van McCreery—and he had the only pair of scissors that could cut hair. So every aspirant to this fashionable cut tried to make interest with Van to fix him up; and Van, who was very good natured, would, as he had time and opportunity, accommodate the applicant, and trim him close. Several of us had gone under the transforming hands of this tonsorial artist, when Bob McIntosh got his turn. Bob was a handsome boy with a luxuriant growth of hair. He had raven black, kinky hair that stuck up from his head in a bushy mass, and he hadn't had his hair cut for a good while, and it was very long and seemed longer than it was because it stuck out so from his head. Now, it was all to go, and a crowd of the boys gathered 'round to see the fun. The modus operandi was simple, but sufficient. The candidate sat on a stump with a towel tied 'round his neck, and he held up the corners making a receptacle to catch the hair as it was cut. Why this—I don't know; force of habit I reckon. When we were boys and our mothers cut our hair, we had to hold up a towel so. We were told it was to keep the hair from getting on the floor and to stuff pincushions with. Here was the whole County of Orange to throw the hair on, and we were not making any pincushions—still Bob had to hold the towel that way. Van stood behind Bob and began over his right ear. He took the hair off clean, as he went, working from right to left over his head; the crowd around—jeering the victim and making comments on his ever-changing appearance as the scissors progressed, making a clean sweep at every cut. We were thus making much noise with our fun at Bob's expense, until the shears had moved up to the top of his head, leaving the whole right half of the head as clean of hair as the palm of your hand, while the other half was still covered with this long, kinky, jet black hair, which in the absence of the departed locks looked twice as long as before—and Bob did present a spectacle that would make a dog laugh. It was just as funny as it could be.

A Surprise Attack

Just at that moment, in the midst of all this hilarity, suddenly we heard a man yell out something as he came running down the hill from the guns. We could not hear what he said. The next moment, he burst excitedly into our midst, and shouted out, "For God's sake, men, get your guns. The Yankees are across the river and making for the guns. They will capture them before you get there, if you don't hurry up."

This was a bolt out of a clear sky—but we jumped to the call. Everybody instantly forgot everything else and raced for the guns. I saw McCreery running with the scissors in his hand; he forgot that he had them—but it was funny to see a soldier going to war with a pair of scissors! I found myself running beside Bob McIntosh, with his hat off, his head half shaved and that towel, still tied round his neck, streaming out behind him in the wind.

Just before we got to the guns, Bob suddenly halted and said, "Good Heavens, Billy, it has just come to me what a devil of a fix I am in with my head in this condition. I tell you now that if the Yankees get too close to the guns, I am going to run. If they got me, or found me dead, they would say that General Lee was bringing up the convicts from the Penitentiary in Richmond to fight them. I wouldn't be caught dead with my head looking like this."

We got to the guns on the hill top and looked to the front. Things were not as bad as that excited messenger had said, but they were bad enough. One brigade of the enemy was across the river and moving on us; another brigade was fording the river; and we could see another brigade moving down to the river bank on the other side. Things were serious, because the situation was this: an Infantry Brigade from Ewell's Corps, lying in winter quarters in the country behind us, was kept posted at the front, whose duty it was to picket the river bank. It was relieved at regular times by another Brigade which took over that duty.

It so chanced that this was the morning for that relieving Brigade to come. Expecting them to arrive any minute, the Brigade on duty, by way of saving time, gathered in its pickets and moved off back toward camp. The other Brigade had not come up—careless work, perhaps, but here in the dead of winter nobody dreamed of the enemy starting anything.

So it was, that, with one brigade gone; the other not up; the pickets withdrawn, at this moment there was nobody whatsoever on the front except our Battery—and, here was the enemy across the river, moving on us and no supports.

In the meantime, the enemy guns across the river opened on us and the shells were flying about us in lively fashion. It was rather a sudden transition from peace to war, but we had been at this business before; the sound of the shells was not unfamiliar—so we were not unduly disturbed. We quickly got the guns loaded, and opened on that Infantry, advancing up the hill. We worked rapidly, for the case was urgent, and we made it as lively for those fellows as we possibly could. In a few minutes a pretty neat little battle was making the welkin ring. The sound of our guns crashing over the country behind us made our people, in the camp back there, sit up and take notice. In a few minutes we heard the sound of a horse's feet running at full speed, and Gen. Dick Ewell, commanding the Second Corps, came dashing up much excited. As he drew near the guns he yelled out, "What on earth is the matter here?" When he got far enough up the hill to look over the crest, he saw the enemy advancing from the river, "Aha, I see," he exclaimed. Then he galloped up to us and shouted, "Boys, keep them back ten minutes and I'll have men enough here to eat them up—without salt!" So saying, he whirled his horse, and tore off back down the road.

In a few minutes we heard the tap of a drum and the relieving Brigade, which had been delayed, came up at a rapid double quick, and deployed to the right of our guns; they had heard the sound of our firing and struck a trot. A few minutes more, and the Brigade that had left, that morning, came rushing up and deployed to our left. They had heard our guns and halted and came back to see what was up.

With a whoop and a yell, those two Brigades went at the enemy who had been halted by our fire. In a short time said enemy changed their minds about wanting to stay on our side, and went back over the river a good deal faster than they came. They left some prisoners and about 300 dead and wounded—for us to remember them by.

The battle ceased, the picket line was restored along the river bank, and all was quiet again. Bob McIntosh was more put out by all this business than anybody else—it had interrupted his hair cut. When we first got the guns into action, everybody was too busy to notice Bob's head. After we got settled down to work, I caught sight of that half-shaved head and it was the funniest object you ever saw. Bob was No. 1 at his gun, which was next to mine, and had to swab and ram the gun. This necessitated his constantly turning from side to side, displaying first this, and then the other side of his head. One side was perfectly white and bare; the other side covered by a mop of kinky, jet black hair; but when you caught sight of his front elevation, the effect was indescribable. While Bob was unconsciously making this absurd exhibition, it was too much to stand, even in a fight. I said to the boys around my gun, "Look at Bob." They looked and they could hardly work the gun for laughing.

Of course, when the fight was over McCreery lost that pair of scissors, or *said* he did. There was not another pair in camp, so Bob had to go about with his head in that condition for about a week—and he wearied of life. One day in his desperation, he said he wanted to get some of that hair off his head so much that he would resort to any means. He had tried to cut some off with his knife. One of the boys, Hunter Dupuy, was standing by chopping on the level top of a stump with a hatchet. Hunter said, "All right, Bob, put your head on this stump and I'll chop off some of your hair." The blade was dull, and it only forced a quantity of the hair down into the wood, where it stuck, and held Bob's hair fast to the stump, besides pulling out a lot by the roots, and hurting Bob very much. He tried to pull loose and couldn't. Then he began to call Hunter all the names he could think of, and threatened what he was going to do to him when he got loose. Hunter, much hurt by such ungracious return for what he had done at Bob's request, said, "Why, Bob, you couldn't expect me to cut your hair with a hatchet without hurting some"—which seemed reasonable. We made Bob promise to keep the peace, on pain of leaving him tied to the stump—then we cut him loose with our knives.

After some days, when we had had our fun, Van found the scissors and trimmed off the other side of his head to match—Bob was happy.

Wedding Bells and a Visit Home

A few days after this I had the very great pleasure of a little visit to my home. My sister, to whom I was devotedly attached, was to be married. The marriage was to take place on a certain Monday. I had applied for a short leave of absence and thought, if granted, to have it come to me some days before the date of the wedding, so that I could easily get home in time. But there was some delay, and the official paper did not get into my hands until fifteen minutes before one o'clock on Sunday—the day before the wedding. The last train by which I could possibly reach home in time was to leave Orange Court House for Richmond at six o'clock that evening, and the Court House was nineteen miles off. It seemed pretty desperate, but I was bound to make it. I had had a very slim breakfast that morning; I swapped my share of dinner that evening with a fellow for two crackers, which he happened to have, and lit out for the train.

A word about that trip, as a mark of the times, may be worth while. I got the furlough at 12.45. I was on the road at one, and I made that nineteen miles in five hours—some fast travel, that! I got to the depot about two minutes after six; the train actually started when I was still ten steps off. I jumped like a kangaroo, but the end of the train had just passed me when I reached the track. I had to chase the train twenty steps alongside the track, and at last, getting up with the back platform of the rear car, I made a big jump, and managed to land. It was a close shave, but with that nineteen-mile walk behind, and that wedding in front, I would have caught that train if I had to chase it to Gordonsville—"What do you take me for that I should let a little thing like that make me miss the party?"

Well, anyhow, I got on. The cars were crowded—not a vacant seat on the train. We left Orange Court House at six o'clock P. M.—we reached Richmond at seven o'clock the next morning—traveled all night—thirteen hours for the trip, which now takes two and a half hours—and all that long night, there was not a seat for me to sit on—except the floor, and that was unsitable. When I got too tired to stand up any longer, I would climb up and sit on the flat top of the water cooler, which was up so near the sloping top of the car that I could not sit up straight. My back would soon get so cramped that I could not bear it any longer—then I crawled down and stood on the floor again. So I changed from the floor to the water cooler and back again, for change of position, all through the night in that hot, crowded car, and I was very tired when we got to Richmond.

We arrived at seven o'clock and the train—Richmond and Danville Railroad—was to start for Danville at eight. I got out and walked about to limber up a little for the rest of the trip. I had a discussion with myself which I found it rather hard to decide. I had only half a dollar in my pocket. The furlough furnished the transportation on the train, and the question was this—with this I could get a little something to eat, or I could get a clean shave. On the one hand I was very hungry. I had not eaten anything since early morning of the day before, and since then had walked nineteen miles and spent that weary night on the train without a wink of sleep. Moreover, there was no chance of anything to eat until we got to Danville that night—another day of fasting—strong reasons for spending that half dollar in *food*. On the other hand, I was going to a wedding party where I would meet a lot of girls, and above all, was to "wait" with the prettiest girl in the State of Virginia. In those days, the wedding customs were somewhat different from those now in vogue. Instead of a "best man" to act as "bottle holder" to the groom, and a "best girl" to stand by the bride and pull off her glove, and fix her veil, and see that her train hangs right, when she starts back down the aisle with her victim—the custom was to have a number of couples of "waiters" chosen by the bride and groom from among their special friends, who would march up in procession, ahead of the bride and groom, who followed them arm in arm to the chancel.

The "first waiters" did the office of "best" man and girl, as it is now. I have been at a wedding where fourteen couples of waiters marched in the procession.

Well, I was going into such company, and had to escort up the aisle that beautiful cousin, that I was telling you about—naturally I wanted to look my best, and the more I thought about that girl, the more I wanted to, so I at last decided to spend that only fifty cents for a clean shave—and got it. My heart and my conscience approved of this decision, but I suffered many pangs in other quarters, owing to that long fasting day. However, virtue is its own reward, and that night when I got home, and that lovely cousin was the first who came out of the door to greet me, dressed in a—well, white swiss muslin—I reckon—and looking like an angel, I felt glad that I had a clean face.

And after the rough life of camp, what a delicious pleasure it was to be with the people I loved best on earth, and to see the fresh faces of my girl friends, and the kind faces of our old friends and neighbors! I cannot express how delightful it was to be at home—the joy of it sank into my soul. Also, I might say, that at the wedding supper, I made a brilliant reputation as an expert with a knife and fork, that lived in the memory of my friends for a long time. My courage and endurance in that cuisine commanded the wonder, and admiration, of the spectators. It was good to have enough to eat once more. I had almost forgotten how it felt—not to be hungry; and it was the more pleasant to note how much pleasure it gave your friends to see you do it, and not have a lot of hungry fellows sitting around with a wistful look in their eyes.

Well, I spent a few happy days with the dear home folks in the dear old home. This was the home where I had lived all my life, in the sweetest home life a boy ever had. Everything, and every person in and around it, was associated with all the memories of a happy childhood and youth. It was a home to love; a home to defend; a home to die for—the dearest spot on earth to me. It was an inexpressible delight to be under its roof—once more. I enjoyed it with all my heart for those *few short days*—then, with what cheerfulness I could—hied me back to camp—to rejoin my comrades, who were fighting to protect homes that were as dear to them as this was to me.

I made another long drawn-out railroad trip, winding up with that same old nineteen miles from Orange to the camp, and I got there all right, and found the boys well and jolly, but still hungry. They went wild over my graphic description of the wedding supper. The picture was very trying to their feelings, because the original was so far out of reach.

The Soldiers' Profession of Faith

In this account of our life in that winter camp, it remains for me to record the most important occurrence of all. About this time there came into the life of the men of the Battery an experience more deeply impressive, and of more vital consequence to them than anything that had ever happened, or ever could happen in their whole life, as soldiers, and as men. The outward beginning of it was very quiet, and simple. We had built a little log church, or meeting house, and the fellows who chose had gotten into the way of gathering here every afternoon for a very simple prayer meeting. We had no chaplain and there were only a few Christians among the men. At these meetings one of the young fellows would read a passage of Scripture, and offer a prayer, and all joined in singing a hymn or two. We began to notice an increase of interest, and a larger attendance of the men. A feature of our meeting was a time given for talk, when it was understood that if any fellow had anything to say appropriate to the occasion, he was at liberty to say it. Now and then one of the boys did have a few simple words to offer his comrades in connection, perhaps, with the Scripture reading.

One day John Wise, one of the best, and bravest men in the Battery, loved and respected by everybody, quietly stood up and said, "I think it honest and right to say to my comrades that I have resolved to be a Christian. I here declare myself a believer in Christ. I want to be counted as such, and by the help of God, will try to live as such."

This was entirely unexpected. He sat down amidst intense silence. A spirit of deep seriousness seemed fallen upon all present. A hymn was sung, and they quietly dispersed. Some of us shook hands with Wise and expressed our pleasure at what he had said, and done.

This incident produced a profound impression among the men. It brought out the feelings about religion that had lain unexpressed in other minds. The thoughts of many hearts were revealed. The interest spread rapidly; the fervor of our prayer meetings grew. We had no chaplain to handle this situation, but men would seek out their comrades who were Christians, and talk on this great subject with them, and accept such guidance in truth, and duty as they could give. And now from day to day at the prayer meetings men would get up in the quiet way John Wise had done, and in simple words declare themselves Christians in the presence of their comrades. Most of them were among the manliest and best men of the company; they were dead in earnest, and their actions commanded the respect and sympathy of the whole camp.

This movement went quietly on, without any fuss or excitement, until some sixty-five men, two-thirds of our whole number, had confessed their faith, and taken their stand, and in conduct and spirit, as well as in word, were living consistent Christian lives. They carried that faith, and that life, and character, home when they went back after the war—and they carried them through their lives. In the various communities where they lived their lives, and did their work, they were known as strong, stalwart Christian men, and towers of strength to the several churches to which they became attached. Of that number twelve or fourteen men went into the ministry of different churches, and served faithfully to their life's end.

What I have described as going on in our Battery off there by itself at Morton's Ford, was going on very widely in the Army at large. There was a deep spiritual interest and strong revival of religion throughout the whole Army of Northern Virginia during that winter. Thousands and thousands of those splendid soldiers of the South, became just as devoted soldiers, and servants of Jesus Christ, and took their places in His ranks, and manfully fought under His banner, and were not ashamed to confess the faith of Christ crucified, and to stand for His cause.

The effect of all this was very far-reaching. What these men carried back home with them wrought a great change in the South—a change in the attitude of the men of the South toward Christ's religion. There was a great change in that attitude, from before the war, and afterward, produced by the war.

I will try to explain what I mean: Before the war, in the South, as I knew it—in the country neighborhoods, and in the villages, and small towns—you would find a group of men, often made up of the most influential, respected, educated, efficient men of that community, who were not members of any church or professed Christians. These were men of honor and integrity, respected by all, valuable citizens. They respected religion, went to church regularly, as became a gentleman, and gave their money liberally to support the church as a valuable institution of society. That was, their attitude toward religion—respectful tolerance, but no personal interest—no need of it. Their thought, generally unspoken but sometimes expressed, was that religion was all right for women, and children, and sick or weak men, but strong men could take care of themselves and had no need of it. And, of course, the young men coming on were influenced by their example and thought it manly to follow their example. The argument was specious. "There is Mr. Blank; he is an upright, good man, and no man stands higher in the community; he is just as good a man and citizen as any member of the church. He gets along all right without religion—I won't bother about it." So he let it alone and went his way. The very virtues of that group of men were a baleful influence in that community—led young men into the dreadful mistake that men do not need religion—that religion is not a manly thing. A good man who is not a Christian does ten-fold more harm, in a community, to the cause of Christ, and to the lives of men than the worst, and lowest man in it; so it was here!

When the call to war came, these very men were the first to go. As a rule they were the leaders, in thought and action, of their fellow-citizens, and they were high spirited, intensely patriotic, and quick to resent the invasion of their rights, and their State. In whole-hearted devotion to the cause, they went in a spirit that would make them thorough soldiers.

The Example of Lee, Jackson and Stuart

Now when these men got into the army the "esprit de corps" took possession of them. They got shaken down to *soldier* thoughts, and judgments. They began to estimate men by their personal value to the cause that was their supreme concern. In that army, three men held the highest place in the heart and mind, of every soldier in it—they were General Lee, Stonewall Jackson and Jeb Stuart—each the highest in his line. All the army had, for these three men, reverent honor, enthusiastic admiration, and absolute confidence. We looked up to them as the highest types of manhood—in noble character, superb genius, and consummate ability. They were by eminence the heroes—the beloved leaders of the army. There were many other able, and brilliant leaders, whom we honored, but these were set apart. In the thoughts, and hearts of all the army, and the country as well, these three were the noblest and highest representatives of our cause; and every man did homage to them, and was proud to do it. But, as was known, with all their high qualities of genius, and personal character, and superb manhood, each one of these three men was a devout member of Christ's Church; a sincere and humble disciple of Jesus Christ; and in his daily life and all his actions and relations in life, was a consistent Christian man. All his brilliant service to his country was done as duty to his God, and all his plans and purposes were "referred to God, and His approval and blessing invoked upon them, as the only assurance of their success." All who were personally associated with these men came to know that this was the spirit of their lives; and many times, in religious services, in camp, these men, so idolized by the army, and so great in all human eyes but their own, could be seen bowing humbly down beside the private soldiers to receive the holy sacrament of the Blessed Body and Blood of Christ.

Now, when the men, who had been so indifferent to religion at home, as so unnecessary for them, came up against this fact, and came to look up to these three men as their highest ideals of manhood, they got an eye opener. If men like Lee, and Jackson, and Stuart, and others, felt the need of religion for themselves, the thought would come, "Maybe I need it, too. No man can look down on the manhood of these men; if they esteem religion as the crown of their manhood, it is not a thing to be despised, or neglected, or treated with indifference. It is a thing to be sought, and found and taken into my life." And this train of thought arrested the attention, and got the interest and stirred to truer thoughts, and finally brought them to Christ. Thousands of these men were led to become devout Christians, and earnest members of the church through the influence of the three great Christian leaders, and other Christian comrades in the army.

Now, when these men got back home after the war and the survivors of those groups got settled back in their various communities, there was a great difference in the religious situation, from what it had been before the war. There had taken place a complete change in these men, in their attitude toward religion, and this wrought a great change in this respect in their communities, for the returned soldiers of any community were given a place of peculiar honor, and influence. They had their record of splendid, and heroic service behind them and they were held in affectionate, and tender regard — not only by their own families, and friends, but by all their neighbors and fellow-citizens. What that group of soldiers thought, and wanted, *went* in that town, or countryside.

Now, that group of men who set the pace, and made the atmosphere in that community were Christians. The serious phase of life; the seasoning of hardships; the discipline; the oft facing of death; the stern habit of duty at any cost, which they had passed through during the war had made them very strong men, and very earnest Christians. What they stood for, they stood for boldly, and outspokenly on all proper occasions. They were not one whit ashamed of their religion and were ready at all times, and about all matters to let the world know just where they stood; to declare by word, and deed who they were, and whom they served.

All this set up before the eyes of that community a very strong, forcible, manly type of religion. These were not women, and children, and they were not sick or weak men — they were the very manliest men in that town, and so were taken and accepted by general consent.

Just think of the effect of that situation upon the boys and young men growing up in that community. The veteran soldiers, back from the war, with all their honors upon them—were heroes to the young fellows. What the soldiers said, and did, were patterns for them to imitate; and the pattern of Christian life, set up before the youngsters, made religion, and church membership most honorable in their eyes. They did not now, as aforetime, have to overcome the obstacle in a young man's mind which lay in the association of weakness with religion, and which had largely been suggested to them by the older men, in the former times.

The old Christian soldiers, whom they now saw, set up in them the idea that religion was the manliest thing in the world, and so inclined them toward it, and assured the most serious, and respectful consideration of it. Religion could not be put aside lightly, or treated with contempt as unmanly, for those veteran heroes were living it and stood for it, and they were, in their eyes, the manliest men they knew.

Now, this leaven of truer thought about religion was leading society all through the South; the Southern men and boys everywhere were feeling its influence, and it was having most remarkable effects. The increase in the number of men, who after the war were brought into the church by the direct influence of the returned soldiers, "who had found their souls" through the experiences of their army life, was tremendous. Those soldiers did a bigger service to the men of their race by bringing back religion to them than they did in fighting for them during the war.

Just after the war, in the far harder trials and soul agony of the Reconstruction days, I think that the wonderful patience, and courage which resisted humiliation, and won back the control of their States, and rebuilt their shattered fortunes and pulled their country triumphantly up out of indescribable disaster, can only be thus really explained—that those men were "strong and of a good courage" because "their minds were staked on God."

The history of the Southern people during that epoch is unmatched by the history of any people in all time. The result they achieved, this was the reason—beneath the superb "grit" of the Southern people lay deep the conviction "God is our refuge and strength" and "The

God whom we serve. He will deliver us." It was the spiritual vision of the men of the South that saved it when it was ready to perish—and let the men of the South never forget it! Let them give unceasing recognition and thanks to God, for that great deliverance.

If I have made clear my thought—the connection of the religious revival in the army with the fortunes of our people at home after the war—I am glad! If I haven't, I am sorry! I can't say any fairer than that, and I can only make the plea that was stuck up in a church in the West, in the old rough days, when a dissatisfied auditor of the sermon, or the organist, was likely to express his disapproval with a gun. The notice up in front of the choir read like this: "Please don't shoot the musician, he's doing his level best"—I make the same request.

But, to return to our muttons! Let us get back to the winter camp at Morton's Ford.

Spring Sprouts and a "Tar Heel" Story

The winter had now worn away and the spring had come. Vegetation began to show signs of life. Its coming bore us one comfort in one way—among others. It was not so cold, and we did not have to tote so many logs of wood to keep up our fires. Down on the river flats, where vegetation showed sooner than it did on the hills, green things began to shoot up. Dandelions, sheep sorrel, poke leaves and such, though not used in civil life, were welcome to us, for they were much better than no salad at all. The men craved something green. The unbroken diet of just bread and meat—generally salt meat at that—gave some of the men scurvy. The only remedy for that was something acid, or vegetable food. The men needed this and craved it—so when the green shoots of any kind appeared we would go down on the flats, and gather up all the green stuff we could find, and boil it with the little piece of bacon we might have. It improved the health of the men very much.

At this time, there was a North Carolina Brigade of Infantry at the front furnishing pickets for the river bank. They were camped just back of our winter quarters. Those fellows seemed to be very specially strong in their yearning for vegetable diet, so much so that they attracted our attention. Every day we would see long lines of those men passing through our camp. They would walk along, one behind another, in almost unending procession, silent and lonesome, never saying a word and never two walking together—and all of them meandered along intent on one thing—getting down to the flats below "to get some sprouts" as they would say when asked where they were going.

Later on, we would see them in the same solemn procession coming back to camp—every man with a bunch of something green in his fist.

This daily spectacle of Tar Heels swarming through our camp interested us; we watched them mooning along. We tried to talk with them, but all we got from them was, "We'uns is going to git some sprouts. Don't you'uns love sprouts?"

We did, but we didn't go after them in such a solemn manner. Our "sprout" hunts were not so funereal a function; rather more jovial, and much more sociable. Also this devotion to the search for the herb of the field excited our curiosity. They were all the time craving green stuff, and going after it so constantly. We had a story going around which was supposed to explain the craving of a Tar Heel's insides for greens.

This was the story:

One of these men got into the hospital. He had something the matter with his liver. The doctor tried his best to find out what was the matter, and tried all sorts of remedies—no results. At last, in desperation, the doctor decided to try heroic treatment. He cut the fellow open, took out his liver, fixed it up all right (whatever that consisted in), washed it off and hung it on a bush to dry, preparatory to putting it back in place. A dog stole the liver, and carried it off. Here was a bad state of things—the soldier's liver gone, the doctor was responsible. The doctor was up against it. He thought much, and anxiously. At last a bright idea struck him. He sent off, got a sheep, killed it, took out its liver, got it ready, and sewed it up in that soldier in place of his own. The man got well, and about his duties again. One day, soon after, the doctor met him and said with much friendly interest, "Well, Jim, how are you?"

"Oh, doctor," he replied in a very cheerful tone, "I'm well and strong again."

The doctor looked at him, and asked him significantly, "Jim, do you feel *all right*?"

Falling into that characteristic whine, Jim said, "Yes, sir, I am well and strong, but, Doctor, all the time, now, I feel the strangest hankering after grass."

That was the sheep's liver telling. Our theory was that all of those fellows had sheep's livers, and that accounted for the insatiable "hankering after grass."

I told this story in an after-dinner speech at a banquet some time ago to a company of twenty-nine female doctors of medicine—trained, and practicing physicians. They made no protest; listened with unbroken gravity; accepted it as a narrative of actual occurrence, and looked at me with wide-eyed interest. When I finished I thought it best to tell them that it was all a joke. Then they laughed themselves into a fit.

Well, this little account of our doings, and our life in the winter camp at Morton's Ford—1863-1864—is done. Out of its duties, and companionships; its pleasures, and its deeper experiences, we Howitzers were laying up pleasant memories of the camp for the years to come. And often in after years, when some of us comrades got together we would speak of the old camp at Morton's Ford.

The spring was now coming on. We knew that our stay here could not last much longer. How, and when, and where we should go from here, we did not know. We knew we would go somewhere—that was all. "We would know when the time came, and 'Marse Robert' wanted us" he would tell us.

That is the soldier's life—"Go, and he goeth; come, and he cometh; do this, and he doeth it." No choice. Wait for orders—then, quick! Go to it!

Well we were perfectly willing to trust "Marse Robert" and perfectly ready to do just what he said. Meantime we take no anxious thought for the morrow; we go on with our work, and our play—we are "prepared to move at a moment's warning."

CHAPTER II

BATTLE OF THE WILDERNESS

Nineteen miles from Orange Court House, Virginia, the road running northeast into Culpeper crosses "Morton's Ford" of the Rapidan River, which, just now, lay between the Federal "Army of the Potomac" and the Confederate "Army of Northern Virginia."

As this road approaches within three-fourths of a mile of the river it rises over a sharp hill, and, thence, winds its way down the hill to the Ford. On the ridge, just where the road crosses it, the guns of the "First Richmond Howitzers" were in position, commanding the Ford; and the Howitzer Camp was to the right of the road, in the pine wood just back of the ridge. Here, we had been on picket all the winter, helping the infantry pickets to watch the enemy and guard the Ford.

One bright sunny morning, the 2d of May, 1864, a courier rode into the Howitzer Camp. We had been expecting him, and knew at once that "something was up." The soldier instinct and long experience told us that it was about time for something to turn up. The long winter had worn away; the sun and winds, of March and April, had made the roads firm again. Just across the river lay the great army, which was only waiting for this, to make another desperate push for Richmond, and we were there for the particular purpose of making that push vain.

For some days we had seen great volumes of smoke rising, in various directions, across the river, and heard bands playing, and frequent volleys of firearms, over in the Federal Camp. Everybody knew what all this meant, so we had been looking for that courier.

Soon after we reached the Captain's tent, orders were given to pack up whatever we could not carry on the campaign, and in two hours, a wagon would leave, to take all this stuff to Orange Court House; thence it would be taken to Richmond and kept for us, until next winter.

This was quickly done! The packing was not done in "Saratoga trunks," nor were the things piles of furs and winter luxuries. The "things" consisted of whatever, above absolute necessaries, had been accumulated in winter quarters; a fiddle, a chessboard, a set of quoits, an extra blanket, or shirt, or pair of shoes, that any favored child of Fortune had been able to get hold of during the winter. Everything like this must go. It did not take long to roll all the "extras" into bundles, strap them up and pitch them into the wagon. And in less than two hours after the order was given the wagon was gone, and the men left in campaign "trim."

This meant that each man had, left, one blanket, one small haversack, one change of underclothes, a canteen, cup and plate, of tin, a knife and fork, and the clothes in which he stood. When ready to march, the blanket, rolled lengthwise, the ends brought together and strapped, hung from left shoulder across under right arm, the haversack,—furnished with towel, soap, comb, knife and fork in various pockets, a change of underclothes in one main division, and whatever rations we happened to have, in the other,—hung on the left hip; the canteen, cup and plate, tied together, hung on the right; toothbrush, "at will," stuck in two button holes of jacket, or in haversack; tobacco bag hung to a breast button, pipe in pocket. In this rig,—into which a fellow could get in just two minutes from a state of rest,—the Confederate Soldier considered himself all right, and ready for anything; in this he marched, and in this he fought. Like the terrapin—"all he had he carried on his back"—this *all* weighed about seven or eight pounds.

The extra baggage gone, all of us knew that the end of our stay here was very near, and we were all ready to pick up and go; we were on the eve of battle and everybody was on the "qui vive" for decisive orders. They quickly came!

"Marse Robert" Calls to Arms

On the next day but one, the 4th, about 10 o'clock, another courier galloped into camp, and, in a few moments, everybody having seen him, all the men had swarmed up to the Captain's tent to hear the first news. Captain McCarthy came toward us and said, very quietly, "Boys, get ready! we leave here in two hours." Then the courier told us that "Grant was crossing below us in the wilderness. That everything we had was pushing down to meet him; and that Longstreet, lately back from Tennessee, was at Gordonsville." The news telling was here interrupted by Crouch sounding the familiar bugle call—"Boots and saddles," which, to artillery ears, said, "Harness up, hitch up and prepare to move at a moment's warning."

From the Rapidan to Richmond and the Spottsylvania Campaign

The fellows instantly scattered, every man to his quarters, and for a few minutes nothing could be seen but the getting down and rolling up of "flys" from over the log pens they had covered, rolling up blankets, getting together of each man's traps where he could put his hands on them. The drivers took their teams up on the hill to bring down the guns from their positions. All was quickly ready, and then we waited for orders to move.

It was with a feeling of sadness we thought of leaving this spot! It had been our home for several months; it was painful to see it dismantled, and to think that the place, every part of which had some pleasant association with it, would be left silent and lonely, and that we should see it no more.

While we waited, after each had bidden a sad "good-bye" to his house, and its endeared surroundings, it was suggested that we gather once more, for a last meeting in our log church. All felt that this was a fitting farewell to the place. To many of us this little log church was a sacred place, many a hearty prayer meeting had been held there; many a rousing hymn, that almost raised the roof, many a good sermon and many a stirring talk had we heard; many a manly confession had been declared, many a hearty, impressive service in the solemn Litany of the Church, read by us, young Churchmen, in turn. To all the Christians of the Battery (they now numbered a large majority) this church was sacred. To some, it was very, very sacred, for in it they had been born again unto God. Here they had been led to find Christ, and in the assemblies of their comrades gathered here, they had, one after another, stood up and, simply, bravely, and clearly, witnessed a "good confession" of their Lord, and of their faith.

So, we all instantly seized on the motion, to gather in the church. A hymn was sung, a prayer offered for God's protection in the perils we well knew, we were about to meet. That He would help us to be brave men, and faithful unto death, as Southern soldiers; that He would give victory to our arms, and peace to our Country. A Scripture passage, the 91st Psalm, declaring God's defense of those who trust Him, was read. And then, our "talk meeting." It was resolved that "during the coming campaign, every evening, about sunset, whenever it was at all possible, we would keep up our custom, and such of us as could get together, *wherever we might be*, should gather for prayer."

And, in passing, I may remark, as a notable fact, that this resolution was carried out *almost literally*. Sometimes, a few of the fellows would gather in prayer, while the rest of us fought the guns. Several times, to my *very lively* recollection we met *under fire*. Once, I remember, a shell burst right by us, and covered us with dust; and, once, I recall with *very particular* distinctness, a Minie bullet slapped into a hickory sapling, against which I was sitting, not an inch above my head. Scripture was being read at the time, and the fellows were sitting around with their eyes open. I had to *look* as if I had as lieve be there, as anywhere else; but I *hadn't*, by a large majority. I *could* not dodge, as I was sitting down, but felt like drawing in my backbone until it telescoped.

But, however circumstanced, in battle, on the battle line, in interims of quiet, or otherwise, we held that prayer hour nearly every day, at sunset, during the entire campaign. And some of us thought, and *think* that the strange exemption our Battery experienced, our little loss, in the midst of unnumbered perils, and incessant service, during that awful campaign, was, that, in answer to our prayers, "the God of battles covered our heads in the day of battle" and was merciful to us, because we "called upon Him." If any think this a "fond fancy" *we don't*.

Well! to get back! After another hymn, and a closing prayer, we all shook hands, and then, we took a regretful leave of our dear little Church, and wended our way, quiet and thoughtful, to the road where we found the guns standing, all ready to go. Pretty soon the command—"Forward!" rang from the head of the line. We fell in alongside our respective guns, and with a ringing cheer of hearty farewell to the old Camp, we briskly took the road,—to meet, and to do, what was before us.

We tramped along cheerily until about dark, when we bivouacked on the side of the road, with orders to start at daylight next morning. As we pushed along the road,—what road! gracious only knows, but a country road bearing south toward Verdiersville,—brigades, and batteries joined our march, from other country roads, by which we found that all our people were rapidly pushing in from the camps and positions they had occupied during the winter, and the army was swiftly concentrating.

It was very pleasant to us to get into the stir of the moving army again, as we had been off, quite by ourselves, during the winter, and the greetings and recognitions that flew back and forth as we passed, or were passed by, well known brigades or batteries, were hearty and vociferous. Such jokes and "chaffing" as went on! As usual, every fellow had his remark upon everything and everybody he passed. Any peculiarity of dress or appearance marked out a certain victim to the witty gibes of the men, which had to be escaped from, or the victim had to "grin and bear it." If "Puck" or "Punch" could have marched with a Confederate column once, they might have laid in a stock of jokes and witticisms,—and first-class ones, too,—for use the rest of their lives.

Next morning, at daylight,—the 5th of May,—we promptly pulled out, and soon struck the highway, leading from Orange Court House to Fredericksburg, turned to the left and went sweeping on toward "The Wilderness."

The Spirit of the Soldiers of the South

Here we got into the full tide of movement. Before and behind us the long gray columns were hurrying on to battle,—and as merry as crickets.

One thing that shone conspicuous here, and always, was the indomitable *spirit* of the "Army of Northern Virginia," their intelligence about military movements; their absolute confidence in General Lee, and their quiet, matter of course, *certainty of victory*, under him. Here they were pushing right to certain battle, the dust in clouds, the sun blazing down, hardly anything to eat, and yet, with their arms and uniform away, a spectator might have taken them for a lot of "sand-boys on a picnic," *if* there had only been some eatables along, to give color to this delusion.

And their intelligence! These men were not parts of a great machine moving blindly to their work. Very far from it! Stand on the roadside, as they marched by and hear their talk, the expression of their opinions about what was going on, you soon found that these men, privates, as well as officers, were well aware of what they were doing, and where they were going. In a general way, they knew what was going on, and what was *going to go on*, with the strangest accuracy. By some quick, and wide diffusion of intelligence among the men, they understood affairs, and the general situation perfectly well. For instance, as we passed on down that road to the fight, we knew,—just *how* we didn't know,—but we *did know*, and it was commonly talked of and discussed, as ascertained fact, among us as we marched,—that General Grant had about 150,000 men moving on us. We knew that Longstreet was near Gordonsville, and that one Division of A. P. Hill had not come up. We knew that we had, along with us there, only Ewell's Corps and two divisions of A. P. Hill's Corps, the cavalry and some of Longstreet's artillery. In short, as I well remember, it was a fact, accepted among us, that General Lee was pushing, as hard as he could go, for Grant's 150,000 with about 35,000 men; and yet, knowing all this, these lunatics were sweeping along to that appallingly unequal fight, cracking jokes, laughing, and with not the least idea in the world of anything else but victory. I did not hear a despondent word, nor see a dejected face among the thousands I saw and heard that day. I bear witness to this fact, which I wondered at then, and wonder at now. It is one of the most stirring and touching of my memories of the war. It was the grandest moral exhibition I ever saw! For it was simply the absolute confidence in themselves and in their adored leader. They had seen "Marse Robert" ride down that road, they knew he was at the front, and that was all they *cared* to know. The thing was *bound* to go right—"Wasn't Lee there?" And the devil himself couldn't keep them from going where Lee went, or where he wanted them to go. God bless them, living, or dead, for their loyal faith, and their heroic devotion!

Peace Fare and Fighting Rations!

I have alluded to rations; they were scarce here, as always when any fighting was on hand. Even in camp, where all was at its best, we had for rations, per day, one and a half pints of flour, or coarse cornmeal,—ground with the *cob* in it we used to think,—and one-quarter of a pound of bacon, or "mess pork," or a pound, far more often half a pound, of beef.

But, in time of a fight! Ah then, thin was the fare! That small ration dwindled until, at times, eating was likely to become a "lost art." I have seen a man, Bill Lewis, sit down and eat three days' rations at one time. He said "He did not want the trouble of carrying it, *and* he did want *one* meal occasionally that wasn't an empty form." The idea seemed to be that a Confederate soldier would *fight* exactly in proportion as he *didn't eat*. And his *business* was to *fight*. This theory was put into practice on a very close and accurate calculation; with the odds that, as a rule, we had against us, in the battles of the Army of Northern Virginia, we had to meet two or three to one. Then, each Confederate soldier was called upon to be equal to two or three Federal soldiers, and, therefore, each Confederate must have but *one-half* or *one-third* the rations of a Federal soldier. It was easy figuring, and so it was arranged in practice.

From the Rapidan to Richmond and the Spottsylvania Campaign

It was eminently so in this campaign, from the first. When we left camp, on the 4th a few crackers and small piece of meat were given us, and devoured at once. That evening, and on this day, the 5th, we received *none at all*, and in that hard, forced march we became very hungry. An incident that occurred will show how hungry we were. As we passed the hamlet of Verdiersville, I noticed a little negro boy, black as the "ace of spades" and dirty as a pig, standing on the side of the road gazing with staring eyes at the troops, and holding in his hand a piece of ash-cake, which he was eating. A moment after I passed him, our dear old comrade and messmate, Dr. Carter, the cleanest and most particular man in the army, came running after us (Carter Page, John Page, George Harrison, and myself) with gleeful cries, "Here, fellows, I've got something. It isn't much, but it will give us a bite apiece. Here! look at this, a piece of bread! let me give you some."

As he came up he held in his hand the identical piece of bread I had seen the little darkey munching on. It was a small, wet, half-raw fragment of corn ash-cake, and it had moulded on one edge a complete cast of that little nigger's mouth, the perfect print of every tooth. The Doctor had bought it from him for fifty cents, and now, wanted to divide it with us four—a rather heroic thought that was, in a man hungry as a wolf. Of course we young fellows flatly refused to divide it, as we knew the Doctor, twice our age, needed it more than we. We said, "We were not hungry; couldn't eat anything to save us." A lie, that I hope the recording Angel, considering the motive, didn't take down; or, if he did, I hope he added a note explaining the circumstances.

We then began to joke the Doctor about the print of the little darkey's teeth on his bread and suggested to him, to break off that part. "No, indeed," said the Doctor, gloating over his precious ash-cake, "Bread's too scarce, *I* don't mind about the little nigger's teeth, I can't spare a crumb." And when he found he could not force us to take any, he ate it all up.

Indifference to the tooth prints was a perfectly reasonable sentiment, under the circumstances, and one in which we all would have shared, for we were wolfish enough to have eaten the "little nigger" himself. The Doctor didn't mind the little chap's tooth marks *then* but—he did *afterwards*. After he had been pacified with a square meal, the idea wasn't so pleasant, and though we often recalled the incident, afterwards, the Doctor could not remember *this part of it*.

From the Rapidan to Richmond and the Spottsylvania Campaign

He remembered the piece of ash-cake, but, somehow, he could not be brought to recall the tooth marks in it. Not he!

It was about eleven o'clock when we passed Verdiersville. Soon after, we turned down a road, which led over to the plank road on which A. P. Hill's column was moving. Hour after hour all the morning, reports had come flying back along the columns, that our people, at the front, had seen nothing but Federal Cavalry; hadn't been able to unearth any infantry at all. An impression began to get about that maybe after all, there had been a mistake, and that Grant's army was not in front of us.

About this time, that impression was suddenly and entirely dispelled. A distinct rattle of musketry broke sharply on our ears, and we knew, at once, that we had found *something*, and, in fact, it was soon clear that we had found Federal infantry, enough and to spare.

That sudden outbreak of musketry quickened every pulse, and every step too, in our columns. Harder than ever we pushed ahead, and as we advanced, the firing grew louder, and the volume heavier till it was a long roar. The long-roll beat in our marching columns, and some of the infantry brigades broke into the double quick to the front, and we could see them heading off, right and left into the woods.

Marse Robert's Way of Making One Equal to Three

We had now come to the edge of that forest and thicket-covered district, the "Wilderness of Spottsylvania."

Grant had crossed the Rapidan into this tangled chaparral, and it is said he was very much surprised that Lee did not dispute the passage of the river. But "Ole Marse Robert" had cut too many eye teeth to do anything like that. He was far too deep a file, to stop his enemy from getting himself into "a fix." He knew that when Grant's great army got over there, they would be "entangled in the land, the wilderness would shut them in."

In that wilderness, three men were not three times as many as one man. No! no! not at all! Quite the reverse! Lee wouldn't lift a finger to keep Grant from getting *into* the wilderness, but quick as a flash he was, to keep him from getting out. This, was why he had been marching the legs off of us, rations or no rations. This, was why he couldn't wait for Longstreet, but tore off with the men he had, to

From the Rapidan to Richmond and the Spottsylvania Campaign

meet Grant and fight him, before he could disentangle himself from The Wilderness. We had got up in time; and into the chaparral our men plunged to get at the enemy, and out of it was now roaring back over our swift columns the musketry of the advance. As brigade after brigade dashed into line of battle the roar swelled out grander, and more majestic, until it became a mighty roll of hoarse thunder, which made the air quiver again, and seemed to shake the very ground. The battle of The Wilderness was begun, in dead earnest.

The crushing, pealing thunder kept up right along, almost unbroken, hour after hour, all through the long noon, and longer evening, until just before night, it slackened and died away. It was the most *solemn* sound I ever heard, or ever expect to hear, on earth. I never heard anything like it in any other battle. Nothing could be seen, no movements of troops, in sight, to distract attention, or rivet one's interest on the varying fortunes of a battlefield. Only,—out of the dark woods, which covered all from sight, rolled upward heavy clouds of battle-smoke, and outward, that earth shaking thunder, now and then fiercely sharpened by the "rebel yell,"—the scariest sound that ever split a human ear,—as our men sprang to the death grapple.

We had pushed up along with the rest; but by and by our guns were ordered to halt, to let the infantry go by. Here, while we waited for them to pass, we saw the first effects of the fight. Just off the road there was a small open field containing a little farmhouse and garden and apple orchard, where the cavalry had been at work, that morning before we came up. Around the house and in the orchard lay ten dead Federal troops, three of our men, and a number of horses; all lying as they had fallen. One of the Federals was lying with one leg under his horse, and the other over him; both had, apparently, been instantly killed by the same ball, which had gone clear through the heads of both man and horse. They had fallen together, the man hardly moved from his natural position in the saddle. Another had a sword thrust through his body, and two others, in their terribly gashed heads, gave evidence that they had gone down under the sabre. The rest of them, and all three of our men, had been killed by balls. Not a living thing was seen about the place.

We were called away from this ghastly scene by the guns starting again, and we moved on rapidly to the front. As we went, at a trot, one of the men, John Williams, who was sick with the heat and exhaustion of the trying march, and was sitting on the trail of the gun, suddenly fainted, and fell forward under the wheel. He was, fortunately, saved from instant death by a stone, just in front of which he fell. The ponderous wheel, going so rapidly, struck the stone, and was bounded over his body, only bruising him a little. It was a close shave, but we were spared the loss of a dear comrade, and good soldier.

An Infantry Battle

When we got up pretty close to the line of battle, we halted and then were ordered to pull out beside the road and wait for orders. Here we found a great many batteries parked, and we heard that it was, as yet, impossible to get artillery into action where the infantry was fighting. In fact, the battle of The Wilderness was almost exclusively an *Infantry* fight. But few cannon shots were heard at all during the day; the guns could not be gotten through the thickets. We heard, at the time, that we had only been able to put in two guns, and the Federals, three, and that our people had taken two of them, and the other was withdrawn. Certainly we hardly heard a single shot during most of the fight. But we didn't know at the time the exemption we were to enjoy. It was a strange and unwonted sight, all those guns, around us, idle, with a battle going on. For the way General Lee fought his artillery was a caution to cannoneers. He always put them in, everywhere, and made the fullest use of them. We always expected, and we always got, our full share of any fighting that was going on. And to be idle here, while the musketry was rolling, was entirely a novel sensation. We were under a dropping fire, and we expected to go in every moment. A position which every old soldier will recognize as more trying than being in the thick of a fight. It was very far from soothing.

When we had been waiting here a few minutes, Dr. Newton, since the Rev. John B. Newton of Monumental Church, Richmond, Va., afterwards Bishop Coadjutor of Virginia, but then the surgeon of the 40th Virginia Infantry, rode by our guns, and recognizing several of us, boys, his kinsmen, stopped to speak to us. After a few kind words, as he shook hands with us very warmly at parting, he pointed to his field hospital, hard by, and very blandly said, "Boys, I'll be right here, and I will be glad to do anything for you in my line." To fellows going, as we thought, right into battle, this was about the last kind of talk we wanted to hear. A doctor's offer of service in our situation, was full of ghastly suggestions. So his well-meaning proffer was met with opprobrious epithets, and indignant defiance. It was shouted to him in vigorous Anglo-Saxon, what we thought of doctors anyhow, and that if he didn't look sharp we'd fix him so he would need a doctor, himself, to patch him up. The Doctor rode off laughing at the storm his friendly remarks had raised. Never was a kind offer more ungraciously received. I suppose, however, if any of us had got hurt just then, we would have been glad enough to fall in with the Doctor, and to have his skillful care. Fact is, soldiers are very like citizens—set light by the doctor when *well*, but mighty glad to see him when anything is the matter.

The Doctor, and all his brother "saw-bones" soon had enough to do for other poor fellows, if not for us. Numbers of wounded men streamed past us, asking the way to the hospitals, some, limping painfully along, some, with arms in a sling, some, with blood streaming down over neck or face, some, helped along by a comrade, some, borne on stretchers. It was a battered looking procession; and yet, I suppose that people will be surprised to hear, it was as *cheerful* a lot of fellows, as you can imagine. Wounded men coming from under fire are, as a rule, cheerful, often jolly. Being able to get, honorably, from under fire, with the mark of manly service to show, is enough to make a fellow cheerful, even with a hole through him. Of course I am speaking now of the wounded who can walk, and are not utterly disabled.

Eagerly we stopped those wounded men to ask how the fight was going. Their invariable account was that it was all right. They spoke about what heavy columns the enemy was putting in, but they said we were pressing them back, and every one spoke of the dreadful carnage of the Federals. One fellow said, after he was shot in the advancing line, he had to come back over a place, over which there had been very stubborn fighting, and which our men had carried, like a hurricane at last, and as he expressed it, "Dead Yankees were *knee deep* all over about four acres of ground." The blood was running down and dropping, very freely, off this man's arm, while he stood in the road and told us this.

These accounts of the wounded men from the line of battle put us in good heart, which was not lessened by a long line of Federal prisoners being marched to the rear, and the assurance by one of the guard that there were "plenty more where these came from."

And so at last this long exciting day wore away. As dark fell the firing ceased. We got some wood and made fires, and, pretty soon after, "old Tom Armistead," our Commissary Sergeant, rode up. His appearance was hailed with delight, as the promise of something to eat. These transports were destined to be moderated when Tom told what he had to say. He had ridden on from the wagons, far in the rear, and all he could get was a few crackers, and a small bag of wet brown sugar. This he had brought with him, across his horse.

Each man got two crackers and one handful of sugar. This disappeared in a twinkling. And then we sat around the fires discussing the events of the day. One subject of general anxiety, I remember, was when Longstreet would be up. As well as things had gone this day, we all knew well, how much his Corps would be needed for tomorrow's work. It was generally regarded as certain that he would get up during the night, and we lay down to sleep around our guns confident that all was well for tomorrow.

Next morning we were up early. I don't remember that we had anything to eat, and as the getting anything to eat in those days made a deep impression on our minds, I infer that we didn't. However we got a *wash*, a small one. We did not always enjoy this refreshment; then had to be content with a "dry polish" such as Mr. Squeers recommended to Nicholas Nickelby at "Dotheboys Hall," when the pump froze. But on this occasion we had, with difficulty, secured one canteen of water between three of us, wherein we were better off than some of the others. The tin pan in which we luxuriated during winter quarters had been relegated to the wagon, both as inconvenient to carry, and as requiring too much water. It always took two to get a "campaign wash." One fellow poured a little water, out of the canteen, into his comrade's hands, with which he moistened his countenance, a little more poured over his soaped hands, and the deed was done. On this occasion when one canteen had to serve for three, and no more water was to be had, our ablutions were light; in fact, it was little more than a pantomime, in which we "went through the motions" of a wash. But we were afraid to leave the guns a minute, after daylight, for fear of a sudden movement to the front, so we had to do with what we had.

Soon after this, our cares about all these smaller matters suddenly fell out of sight. That fierce musketry broke out again along the lines, in the woods, in front. It increased in fury, especially on the right. Very soon reports began to float back that the Federals were heavily overlapping A. P. Hill's right, and things looked dangerous. Then it was rumored that some of Hill's right regiments were beginning to give way, under the resistless weight of the columns hurled upon him and round his flank. We could quickly perceive this to be true by the sound of the firing, which came nearer to us and passed toward the left. This immediately threw our crowd into a fever of excitement; the idea of lying there, doing nothing, when our men were falling back, was intolerable. Every artillery man thought that if *his battery* could only get in, it would be all right. We knew what a difference it would instantly make, if all these silent guns could be sweeping the columns of the enemy. We would soon stop them, we thought! We just ached for orders to come but they did not. Still the news came, "impossible to get artillery in;" and loud and deep were the angry complaints of some, and curses of others, and great the disgust of all at our forced inaction. One fellow near me, voiced the feelings of us all—"If we can't get in there, or Longstreet don't get here pretty quick, the devil will be to pay."

Arrival of the First Corps

In the midst of this anxious and high wrought feeling, an excited voice yelled out, "Look out down the road. Here they come!" We were driven nearly wild with excited joy, and enthusiasm by the blessed sight of Longstreet's advance division coming down the road at a double quick, at which pace, after the news of Hill's critical situation reached them, they had come for two miles and a half. The instant the head of his column was seen the cries resounded on every side, "Here's Longstreet. The old war horse is up at last. It's all right now."

On, the swift columns came! Crowding up to the road, on both sides, we yelled ourselves nearly dumb to cheer them as they swept by. Hearty were the greetings as we recognized acquaintances and friends and old battle comrades in the passing columns. Specially did the "Howitzers" make the welkin ring when Barksdale's Mississippi Brigade passed. This was the brigade to which our battery had long been attached, to which we were greatly devoted, with whom we had often fought, and admired as one of the most splendid fighting corps in the army. And loud was the cheer the gallant Mississippians flung back to the "Howitzers."

Everything broke loose as General Longstreet in person rode past. Like a fine lady at a party, Longstreet was often late in his arrival at the ball, but he always made a sensation and that of delight, when he *got* in, with the grand old First Corps, sweeping behind him, as his train.

This was our own Corps, from which we had been separated for some months. The very sight of the gallant old veterans, as they poured on, was enough to make all hearts perfectly easy. Our feeling of relief was complete and as the Brigades disappeared into the woods in the direction of Hill's breaking right, where the thunder of their still heroic resistance to overwhelming odds was roaring, we all felt, "Thank God! it's all right now! Longstreet is up!"

And it *was* all right. The first brigades as they got up formed, and rushed right in, one after another, to check the advance of the enemy. And as they successively went in we could hear the musketry grow more angry and fierce. Before very long, a crashing peal of musketry broke out with a fury that made what we had been hearing before seem like pop-crackers. Our crowd quickly perceived that the sound was receding from us; at the same time the bullets, — which had been falling over among us entirely too lively to be pleasant to fellows who were not shooting any themselves, — stopped coming. We knew what this meant; Longstreet was putting his Corps in, and they were driving the enemy. Soon, to confirm our ideas, lines of Federal prisoners, from Hancock's Corps, they told us, came by, and Longstreet's wounded began to pass. These fellows told us that our Corps had gone in like a whirlwind, had already recovered Hill's line, gone beyond it, and were forcing the Federals back.

They said Hancock's Corps was doubled up, and being torn to pieces and they thought we would "bag the whole business."

The Love that Lee Inspired in the Men He Led

All this was very nice and we were expressing our delight in the usual way. Just then, an officer rode up who told us a bit of news, that made us feel more like tears than cheers, and put every fellow's heart into his mouth. He said that just before, General Lee had come in an ace of being captured. A body of the enemy had pushed through a gap in our line and unexpectedly come right upon the old General, who was quietly sitting upon his horse. That, these fellows could with perfect ease have taken, or shot him, but that he had quietly ridden off, and the enemy not knowing who it was, made no special effort to molest him.

I wish you could have seen the appalled look that fell on the faces of the men, as they listened to this. Although the danger was past an hour ago, they were as pale and startled and shocked as if it were enacting then. The bare idea of anything happening to General Lee was enough to make a man sick, and I assure you it took all the starch out of us for a few minutes.

From the Rapidan to Richmond and the Spottsylvania Campaign

I don't know how it was, but somehow, it never occurred to us that anything *could* happen to General Lee. Of course, we knew that he was often exposed, like the rest of us. We had seen him often enough under hot fire. And, by the way, I believe that the one only thing General Lee ever did, that the men in this army thought he *ought not to do*, was going under fire. We thought him perfect in motive, deed and judgment; he could do no wrong, could make no mistake, but this,—that he was too careless in the way he went about a battlefield. Three different times, during these very fights, at points of danger, he was urged to leave the spot, as it was "not the place for him." At last he said, "I wish I knew *where my place is* on the battlefield; wherever I go some one tells me *that* is not the place for me."

But, he would go! He wanted to see things for himself, and he wished his men to know, that he was looking after them, both seeing that they did their duty, and *caring* for them. And certainly, the sight of his beloved face was like the sun to his men for cheer and encouragement. Every man thought less of personal danger, and no man thought of *failure* after he had seen General Lee riding along the lines. Nobody will ever quite understand what that old man was to us, his soldiers! What absolute confidence we felt in him! What love and devotion we had, what enthusiastic admiration, what filial affection, we cherished for him. We loved him like a father, and thought about him as a devout old Roman thought of the God of War. Anything happen to him! It would have *broken our hearts*, for one thing, and, we could no more think of the "Army of Northern Virginia" without General Lee, at its head, than we could picture the day without the sun shining in the heavens.

An incident illustrating this feeling was taking place up in the front just about the time we were hearing the news of the General's narrow escape.

As the Texan Brigade of Longstreet's Corps, just come up, dashed upon the heavy ranks of the Federals, they passed General Lee with a rousing cheer. The old General, anxious and excited by the critical moment, thrilling with sympathy in their gallant bearing, started to ride in, with them, to the charge. It was told me the next day by some of the Texans, who witnessed it, that the instant the men, unaware of his presence with them before, saw the General along with them in that furious fire, they cried out in pleading tones—"Go back, General Lee. We swear we won't go on, if you don't go back. You shall not stay here in this fire! We'll charge clear through the wilderness if you will only go back." And they said, numbers of the

From the Rapidan to Richmond and the Spottsylvania Campaign

men crowded about the General, and begged him, with tears, to return, and some caught hold of his feet, and some his bridle rein, and turned his horse round, and led him back a few steps,—all the time pleading with him. And then, the General seeing the feelings of his men, and that he was *actually checking the charge* by their anxiety for him, said, "I'll go, my men, if you will drive back those people," and he rode off, they said, with his head down, and they saw tears rolling down his cheeks. And they said, many of the men were sobbing aloud, overcome by this touching scene. Then with one yell, and the tears on their faces, those noble fellows hurled themselves on the masses of the enemy like a thunderbolt. Not only did they stop the advance, but their resistless fury swept all before it and they followed the broken Federals half a mile. They redeemed their promise to General Lee. Eight hundred of them went in, four hundred, only, came out. They covered with glory that day, not only themselves, who did such deeds, but their leader, who could inspire such feelings at such a moment in the hearts of these men. Half their number fell in that splendid charge, but—they saved the line, and they gloriously redeemed their promise to General Lee—"We'll do all you want, if you will only get out of fire." I cannot think of anything stronger than to say that—This General, and these soldiers, were worthy of each other. There is no higher praise!

As the Brigades of Field's division, that followed the Texans, went in, a little incident took place, which illustrated the irrepressible spirit of fun which would break out everywhere, and which we often laughed at afterwards. General Anderson's Brigade was ahead, followed hard by Benning's Brigade, gallant Georgians all, and led by Brigadiers, of whom nothing better can be said, than that they were worthy to lead them. Among the men General Anderson had somehow got the soubriquet of "Tige" and General Benning enjoyed the equally respectful name of "Old Rock." On this occasion, Anderson was ahead, and as he moved out of sight into the woods, his men began to yell and shout like everything. One of Anderson's men, wounded, blood dropping from his elbow and running down his face, was coming out, when he met General Benning, at the head of his column, pushing in as hard as he could go. As this fellow passed him, taking advantage of his wound to have a little joke, he pointed to the woods in front and called out to the General, "Hurry up 'Old Rock,' 'Tige' has treed a pretty big coon he's got up there; you'd better hurry up or you won't get a smell." The brave old Benning, already hurrying himself nearly to death, flashed around on the daring speaker, and saw at once the streaming blood—

From the Rapidan to Richmond and the Spottsylvania Campaign

"Confound that fellow's impudence," said the disgusted General. "I wish he wasn't wounded, if I wouldn't fix him." The fellow well knew that he could say what he pleased to anybody with that blood-covered face.

I think it was about eleven or twelve o'clock we heard that General Longstreet was badly wounded, and soon after he was brought to the rear, near our guns. With several of the others I went out and had some words with the men who were taking him out. To our grief, we heard them say, that his wound was very dangerous, probably fatal. He had fallen, up there in the woods, on the battle front, fighting his corps, in the full tide of victory. He had broken and doubled up Hancock's Corps, and driven it, with great slaughter back upon their works at the Brock road, and in such rout and confusion, that, as he said, he thought he had another "Bull Run" on them. And if he could have forced on that assault, and gotten fixed on the Brock road, it is thought that Grant's army would have been in great peril. But, just in the thick of it, he was mistaken, while out in front in the woods, for the enemy, and shot, by his own men. His fall was in almost every particular just like "Stonewall" Jackson's, in that same wilderness, one year before. Both were shot by their own men, at a critical moment, in the midst of brilliant success, and in both cases their fall saved the enemy from irretrievable disaster. Longstreet's fall checked the attack, which after an inevitable delay of some hours, was resumed. But the enemy seeing his danger had time to recover, and make disposition to meet it.

"Windrows" of Federal Dead

Again, at four o'clock, after this interval of comparative quiet, the thunder of battle crashed and rolled. General Lee, himself, fought Longstreet's Corps. The attack was fierce, obstinate, and fearfully bloody. Wilkinson, of the Army of the Potomac, an eye-witness of this charge, says, in his book, "Recollections of a Private Soldier": "The Confederate fire resembled the fury of hell in its intensity, and was deadly accurate" and that "the story of this fight could afterwards be read by the windrows of dead men." As to its effect he also says: "We could not check the Confederate advance and they forced us back, and back, and back. The charging Confederates broke through the left of the Ninth Corps and would have cut the army in twain, if not caught on the flank, and driven back. Massed for the attack on the Sixth Corps, they were skillfully launched, and ably led, and they struck with terrific violence against Shaler's and Seymour's Brigades, which were routed, with a loss of four thousand prisoners. The Confederates came within an ace of routing the Sixth Corps. Both their assaults along our line were dangerously near being successful." Such was the description of a brave enemy, an eye-witness of this assault. At last, as dark fell, the fire slackened and died out.

The Battle of the Wilderness was done. Grant was pinned into the thickets, hardly able to stand Lee's attack, no thoroughfare to the front and twenty odd thousand of his men dead, wounded and gone. That was about the situation when dark fell on the 6th of May!

That night we drew off some distance to the right, and lay down, supperless, on the ground around our guns; it was very dark and cloudy and soon began to rain. There had been too much powder burnt around there during the last two days for it to stay clear. And so, as it always did, just after heavy firing, the clouds poured down water through the dark night. Lying out exposed on the untented ground, with only one blanket to cover with, we got soaking wet, and stayed so.

The comfortless night gave way, at last, to a comfortless day—May 7th—gloomy, lowering, and raining, off and on, till late in the evening. During the morning, a little desultory firing was heard in front, and then all was quiet and still. We knew enough to know that Grant's push was over at this point. Some of us had gone up to look at the ground over which Longstreet had driven the enemy yesterday. We knew that the Federal troops could never be gotten back over that awful, corpse-covered ground to attack the men who had driven them. We knew we had to fight somewhere else, but where? By and by, talk began to circulate among the men that Spottsylvania, or around near Fredericksburg, might be the place. Of one thing we were all satisfied, that we would know soon enough.

In this waiting and excited state of mind, the long, long, rainy day wore on, and dark fell again. We had managed to conjure up some very lonesome looking fires out of the wet wood lying about (fence rails were not attainable here in the wilderness), and were engaged in a hot dispute about where the next fighting was to be, which warmed and dried us more than the fires did, when "the winter of our discontent" was made "glorious summer," so to speak, by the news that the wagons had got up, and they were going to issue rations. Tom Armistead made this startling announcement in as bland, and matter of course a tone as if he were in the habit of giving us something to eat *every* day, which he was not, by a great deal.

Tom was the dearest fellow in the world, and the best Commissary in the army, and we all loved him. Many a time when, in the confusion of campaign, the wagon was empty, or was snowed in by an avalanche of wagons, far in the rear, he could be seen struggling up to the front with a bag of crackers, sugar, meat, anything that he had been able to lay hands on, across his horse, so that the boys should not starve entirely. Hunting us up through the woods, or along the battle line, he would ride in among us with his load, and a beaming face, that told how glad he was to have something for us. And when, as too often it was, the whole Commissary business was *"dead busted,"* our afflicted Commissary would tell us there was nothing, with such a rueful visage, that it made us sorry we did not have something to give him, and made us feel our own emptiness all the more, that it seemed to afflict him so.

The present rations were quickly distributed, and as quickly devoured, and not a man was foundered by over-eating! Then we sat around the fires and discussed the news that had been gathered from various sources.

CHAPTER III

BATTLES OF SPOTTSYLVANIA COURT HOUSE

It was just ten o'clock and each man was looking around for the dryest spot to spread his blanket on, when a courier rode up, with pressing orders for us to get instantly on the march. In a few moments, we were tramping rapidly through the darkness, on a road that led, we knew not whither. We were, as we found out afterwards, leading the great race, that General Lee was making for Spottsylvania Court House to head off Grant in his efforts to get out of the Wilderness in his "push for Richmond." We were with the vanguard of the skillful movement, by which Longstreet's Corps was marched entirely around Grant's left flank, to seize the strong line of the hills around Spottsylvania Court House and hold it till the other two Corps could come to our aid.

We marched all night, a hard, forced march over muddy roads, through the damp, close night. Soon after the start from our bivouac, a brigade of infantry had filed into the road ahead of us, and we could hear, behind us on the road, though we could not see for the darkness, the sound of other troops marching. The Brigade ahead of us, we soon found, to our gratification, to be Barksdale's Mississippi Brigade, now under command of General Humphreys, since the gallant Barksdale fell at the head of his storming columns at Gettysburg. This was the Brigade to which we had belonged in the earlier organization of the artillery. It was a magnificent body of men, one of the most thorough fighting corps in the army, as they had showed a hundred times, on the bloodiest fields, and were soon, and often to show again. There was a very strong mutual attachment between the First Richmond Howitzers and Barksdale's Brigade, and we were much pleased to be with them on this march. We mingled with them, as we sped rapidly along, and exchanged greetings, and our several experiences since we had been separated.

The morning of the 8th of May broke, foggy and lowering, and found us still moving swiftly along. The infantry halting for a rest, we passed on ahead, and for some time were marching by ourselves. I well recall the impressions of the scene around us on that early morning march. Our battery seemed all alone on a quiet country road. The birds were singing around us, and it seemed, to us, so sweet! Everybody was impressed by the music of those birds. As the

From the Rapidan to Richmond and the Spottsylvania Campaign

old soldiers will remember, the note of a bird was a sound we rarely heard. The feathered songsters, no doubt, were frightened away, and it was often remarked, that we never saw birds in the neighborhood of camp. So we specially enjoyed the treat of hearing them, now and here, in their own quiet woods, where they had never been disturbed. All was quiet and still and peaceful as any rural scene could be. It seemed to us wondrous sweet and beautiful! All the men were strangely impressed by it. They talked of it to one another. It made our hearts soft, it brought to the mind of many of those weary, war-worn soldiers, other quiet rural scenes, where lay their homes and dear ones, and to which this scene made their hearts go back, in tender memory, and loving imagination. All the eyes did not stay dry as we passed along that road. We talked of this scene many a time long afterwards. And I expect some of the old "Howitzers" still remember that quiet Spottsylvania country road, winding through the woods, on that early Sunday morning, when the birds sang to us, as we hurried on to battle.

Well! the morning wore on, and so did we. By and by, the sun came out through the fog and clouds, and began to make it hot for us. The dampness of the earth made this an easy job. The sun got higher and hotter every minute. The way that close, sultry heat did *roast* us was pitiful. We would have "larded the lean earth as we walked along," except that hard bones and muscles of gaunt men didn't *yield* any "lard" to speak of. The *breakfast* hour was not observed, *i. e.*, not with any ceremony. "Cracker nibbling on the fly" was all the visible reminder of that time-honored custom. We were not there to eat, but, to get to Spottsylvania Court House; and *steps* were more to that purpose than *steaks*, so we omitted the steaks, and put in the steps; and we put them in very fast, and were putting in a great many of them, it appeared to us. At last, just about twelve o'clock our road wound down to a stream, which I think was the *Po*, one of the head waters of the Mattaponi River, and then, we went up a very long hill, a bank, surmounted by a rail fence on the left side of the road, and the woods on the other.

Stuart's Four Thousand Cavalry

Just as we got to the top (our Battery happened just then to be ahead of all the troops, and was the first of the columns to reach the spot), the road came up to the level of the land on the left, which enabled us to see, what, though close by us, had been concealed by the high roadside bank. A farm gate opened into a field, around a farmhouse and outbuildings, and there, covering that field was the whole of Fitz

Lee's Division of Stuart's cavalry. These heroic fellows had for two days been fighting Warren's corps of Federal infantry, which General Grant had sent to seize this very line on which *we* had now arrived. They had fought, mostly dismounted, from hill to hill, from fence to fence, from tree to tree; and so obstinate was their resistance, and so skillful the dispositions of the matchless Stuart, that some thirty thousand men had been forced to take about twenty-six hours to get seven or eight miles, by about forty-five hundred cavalry. But, it was incomparable cavalry, and J. E. B. Stuart was handling it. It was some credit to that Corps to have marched any at all! Thanks to the superb conduct of the cavalry, General Lee's movement had succeeded! We had beaten the Federal column, and were here, before them, on this much-coveted line, and meant to hold it, too.

I note here in passing, that this Spottsylvania business was a "white day" for the cavalry. When the army came to know of what the cavalry had done, and *how they had done it*, there was a general outburst of admiration, — the recognition that brave men give to the brave. Stuart and his men were written higher than ever on the honor roll, and the whole army was ready to take off its hat to salute the cavalry.

And, from that day, there was a marked change in the way the army thought and spoke of the cavalry; it took a distinctly different and higher position in the respect of the Army, for it had revealed itself in a new light; it had shown itself signally possessed of the quality, that the infantry and artillery naturally admired most of all others — *obstinacy* in fight.

As was natural, and highly desirable, each arm of the service had a very exalted idea of its own importance and merit, as compared with the others. In fact the soldier of the "Army of Northern Virginia" filled exactly the Duke of Marlborough's description of the spirit of a good soldier. "He is a poor soldier," said the Duke, "who does not think himself as good and better than any other soldier *of his own army*, and *three times as good* as any man in the army *of the enemy*." That fitted our fellows "to a hair;" each Confederate soldier thought that way.

It was not an unnatural or unreasonable conceit, *considering the facts*. It must be confessed that *modesty* as to their quality as soldiers was not the distinguishing virtue of the men of the Army of Northern Virginia, but, it must be considered, in extenuation that their experience in war was by no means a good school for humility. An

From the Rapidan to Richmond and the Spottsylvania Campaign

old Scotch woman once prayed, "Lord, gie us a gude conceit o' ourselves." There was a certain wisdom in the old woman's prayer! The Army of Northern Virginia soldiers had this "gude conceit o' themselves," without praying for it; certainly, if they did pray for it, their prayer was answered, "good measure, pressed down, shaken together, and running over." They had it abundantly! And it was a tremendous element of power in their "make up" as soldiers. It made them the terrible fighters, that all the world knew they were. It largely explains their recorded deeds, and their matchless achievements.

For instance, here at the Wilderness! What was it that made thirty-five thousand men knowingly and cheerfully march to attack one hundred and fifty thousand men, and stick up to them, and fight them for twenty-four hours, without support or reinforcement? It was their good opinion of themselves; their superb confidence. They felt *able* with thirty-five thousand men, *and General Lee*, to meet one hundred and fifty thousand men, and hold them, till help came; *and didn't they do it*?

Well! they did *that kind of thing so often* that they couldn't get humble, and *they never have been able to get humble since*. They *try to*—but—*they can't*!

But I return from this digression to say, that the different Arms of the service had something of this same feeling, this good opinion of themselves, as compared with one another. Each one had many jokes on the others, and whenever they met, all sorts of "chaffing" went on. In all this, the infantry and artillery felt closer together, and were rather apt, when the occasion offered, to turn their combined guns on the cavalry.

The general point of the jokes and gibes at the cavalry was their *supposed* tendency to be *"scarce"* when *big fighting* was going on.

It wasn't that anybody doubted the *usefulness* of cavalry, but their usefulness was imagined to lie in other respects than fighting back the masses of the enemy. And, it wasn't that anybody supposed that the cavalry did not have plenty of fight in them, *if they could get a chance*. We knew that when they were at home they were the same stock as we were, and we believed, that if they were along with us, they would do as well; but in the cavalry, well! we didn't know!

The leaders of the cavalry, Stuart, Hampton, Ashby, Fitz Lee and others, were heroes and household names to the whole army. Their brilliant courage and dare-deviltry, their hairbreadth escapes, and thrilling adventures, their feats of skill, and grace were themes of pride and delight to us all. These cavaliers were the "darlings of the army." *Still*, the army would guy the cavalry every chance they got.

It was said that Gen. D. H. Hill proposed to offer a "reward of Five Dollars, to anybody who could find a dead man with spurs on." And Gen. Jubal Early once, when impatient at the conduct of certain troops in his command threatened "if the cavalry did not do better, he would put them *in the army*."

One day, an infantry brigade on the march to Chancellorsville had halted to rest on the pike, near where a narrow road turned off. A cavalryman was seen approaching, in a fast gallop, plainly, in a great hurry. The infantry viewed his approach with great interest, prepared to salute him with neat and appropriate remarks as he passed, by way of making him lively.

Just before he got to the head of the brigade he reached the narrow road and started up it. Instantly a dozen "infants" began to wave their arms excitedly, and shout in loud earnest voices—"Mister, stop there! don't go a step farther; for heaven's sake *don't* go up that road." The trooper, startled by this appeal, and the warning gestures of the men, approaching him, pulled in his fast-going horse, and stopped, very impatiently. He said in a sharp tone, "What is the matter, why mustn't I go up this road? Say quick, I'm in a big hurry." "Don't go, we beg you; you'll never come back alive." "Humph! is that so?" said this trooper (who had been near breaking a blood vessel in his impatience at being stopped, but cooled off a little, at this ominous remark)—"But what's ahead? what's the danger? The road seems quiet?" "Well, Sonny, *that's* the danger. Haven't you heard about it?" "Now, Sonny," was a term of endearment, which from an "infant" always exasperated the feelings of a cavalryman to the last degree; turned the milk of kindness in a horseman's breast into the sourest clabber; and it instantly stirred up this trooper. "Look here men, don't fool with me. Tell me what is the danger up this road," "Well! we thought we ought to let you know, before you expose yourself. General Hill has offered a reward of Five Dollars for a dead man with spurs on, and if you go up that lonesome road some of these here *soldiers* will shoot you to get the reward." "Oh pshaw!" cried the disgusted victim, clapping spurs to his horse, and away he rode, leaving the grinning and delighted "infants" behind, and leaving, too, his *opinion* of them, and their joke, in language that needed no interpreter.

From the Rapidan to Richmond and the Spottsylvania Campaign

This sort of thing was going on, all the time. The infantry and artillery *would* do it. With many, particularly the artillery, who knew better, it was *only joking*, the soldier-instinct to stir up *any* passer-by. But with many, especially the infantry, who were not as much "up to snuff" as the artillery, these gibes at the cavalry expressed a serious, tho' mistaken idea, they had of them. Upon the advance of the enemy, of course, we were accustomed to see cavalrymen hurrying in from the outposts to the rear, to report. So the thoughtless infantry, not considering that this was "part of the large and general plan," got fixed in their minds an association between the two things,—the advance of the enemy, and, the rapid hurrying off to the rear of the cavalry, until they came to have the fixed idea, that the sight of the enemy *always* made a cavalryman "hungry for solitude." They reasoned that, as a mounted man was much better *fixed* for running away than a footman, it was, by so much, natural that he *should* run away, and was, by so much, the more likely to do it.

Also, our orders to move and to go into battle were always brought by horsemen; so the horsemen were thought about as *causing others to fight* instead of *doing it themselves*. So, in short, it came to pass, that this innocent infantry had a dim sort of notion that the chief end of the cavalry was, in battle time, to run away and bring up other people to do the fighting, and in quiet time, to "range" for buttermilk and other delicacies, which the poor footmen never got. Hence the soubriquet of "buttermilk ranger" universally applied to the cavalry by the army.

But, I assure you, that all this was dispelled at once, and for good and all, at Spottsylvania. Here had these gallants gotten down off their horses. They hadn't run *anywhere at all*; didn't want anybody else to come, and fight for them. They had jumped into about five or six times their number of the flower of the Federal infantry. They met them front to front, and muzzle to muzzle. Of course they had to give back; but it was slowly, *very slowly*, and they made the enemy pay, in blood, for every step they gained. They had worried these Federals into a fever, and kept them fooling away nearly twenty-six hours of priceless time; and made Grant's plan *fail*, and made General Lee's plan succeed, and had secured the strong line for our defence.

It was a piece of regular, obstinate, bloody, "bulldog" work. We knew, well as we thought of ourselves, that not the staunchest brigade of our veteran "incomparable" infantry, or battery of our canister-shooting artillery, could have *fought* better, *stood* better, or

From the Rapidan to Richmond and the Spottsylvania Campaign

achieved more, for the success of the campaign. We felt that General Lee,—that the whole army,—"owed the cavalry one," "*several*," in fact. The army, even the infantry, had come to know the cavalry, at last. Obstinacy, toughness, dogged refusal to be driven, was their test of manhood, and this test the cavalry had signally, and *brilliantly* met. Everybody was satisfied, the *cavalry would do, they* were "all right." We couldn't praise them enough, we were proud of them. The remark was even suffered to pass, as nothing to his discredit particularly, that our "Magnus Apollo," General Lee, himself, had once been in the cavalry, and no one resented it *now*. We knew that it was when he was *younger* than now. We, of the "Howitzers," knew very well what arm of the service, and what corps of that arm, the experienced old General would join, if he was enlisting in the Army of Northern Virginia, now, when he knew more than he did. Still! he had been a cavalryman; admit it!

And we all *admired* the cavalry; *honored* the cavalry; *shouted* for the cavalry, from that time! Occasionally, from force of habit, the infantry (the artillery never) would fall from grace at sight of a passing cavalry column, and let fall little attentions, that sounded very like the old-time compliments, but they were not *meant that way*. It was the soldier-instinct to salute pilgrims. Just as, on a village street, if a dog, of any degree, starts to run, every other dog in sight, or hearing, tears off after him in pursuit, and if he can catch up, instantly attacks him,—not that he has anything against the fugitive, but, simply, because he is running by. The act of running past makes him the enemy of his kind. So, I think, the Confederate infantry assailed, with jokes and gibes, *anybody in motion* by their camp, or column. They had nothing against him; they attacked him because he was passing by. "It was their nature to." Of all living men, General Lee, *alone*, was sacred to them in this. The cavalry *always* had their full share, and never suffered for want of notice.

This account of the false idea that prevailed, the fun that came of it, and the way it was dispelled, is part of the history of the time. It went to make up the life in the Army of Northern Virginia; it lives in the recollection of that good old time. No record of that old time would be complete without it. So I make no apology for falling into it, in this informal reminiscence.

At one o'clock on Sunday, the 8th of May, we reached the top of the hill near Spottsylvania Court House and suddenly came upon Stuart's cavalry massed in the yard and field around a farmhouse. They had finished their splendid fight, the van of the army was on the spot to relieve them. They had been withdrawn from confronting the enemy, and were now drawn up here, preparatory to starting off, to overtake Sheridan's raid toward Richmond; which they did, and, at "Yellow Tavern," two days after, many of them, the immortal Stuart at their head, died and saved Richmond.

Greetings on the Field of Battle

I have lingered at that farmhouse gate, at the top of the hill, in this story, very much longer than we did in reality. In fact we didn't linger there at all. Didn't have a chance! For, the moment we came in sight, at that gate leading into the farmhouse, an officer came dashing out from amongst the troops of cavalry, and galloped across the field toward us. The instant this horseman got out of the crowd, we recognized him. That long waving feather, the long auburn beard, that easy, graceful seat on the swift horse,—that was "J. E. B." Stuart, and nobody else! He rode up to the foremost group of us, and pulled up his horse. With bright, pleasant, smiling face, he returned our hearty salute with a touch of his hat, and a cheerful, "Good morning, boys! glad to see you. What troops are these?" "Richmond Howitzers, Longstreet's Corps." "*Good!* anybody else along?" "Infantry close behind." "Good! Well, boys, I'm *very* glad to see you. I've got a little job for you, right now, all waiting for you." Just then the Captain rode up and saluted. "Captain," said the General, saluting pleasantly, "Draw our guns through the gate and stop. I'll want you in ten minutes." And, away he galloped, back toward the cavalry. The guns pulled in through the gate and halted as they were, on the road leading to the house, close by the cavalry.

We seized this sudden chance to see our old friends among the troopers. In every direction our fellows might be seen darting in among the horses, in search of our friends. Loud and hearty were the shouts of greeting as we recognized, or were seen by, those we sought or unexpectedly lighted on. Brothers, met and embraced. Friends greeted friends. Old schoolmates, who had, three years ago, parted at the schoolroom, locked eager, and loving hands, and asked after others, and told what they could. It was a delightful and touching scene, that meeting there on the edge of a bloody field! they coming out, we going in. There were jokes, and laughs, and cheerful words, but, the hand-clasps were very tight, the sudden uprising of tender feelings, at the sight of faces, and the sound of voices, we had not seen nor heard for years, and that we might see and hear no more. The memories of home, or school, and boyhood, suddenly

From the Rapidan to Richmond and the Spottsylvania Campaign

brought back, by the faces linked with them, made the tears come, and the words very kind, and the tones very gentle.

I had several pleasant encounters. Among others, this: I heard a familiar voice sing out, "William Dame, my dear boy, what on earth are you doing here?" I eagerly turned, and in the figure hasting toward me with outstretched hand,—as soon as I could read between the lines of mud on him,—I recognized my dear old teacher, Jesse Jones. I loved him like an older brother, and was delighted to meet him. I had parted from him, that sad day, three years ago, when our school scattered to the war. I had seen him last, the quiet gentleman, the thoughtful teacher, the pale student, the pink of neatness. Here I find him a dashing officer of the Third Virginia Cavalry, girt with saber and pistols, covered with mud from the crown of his head to the soles of his feet, and just resting from the bloody work of the last two days.

Just here, I had the great pleasure of falling in with my kinsman, and almost brother, Lieut. Robert Page, of the Third Virginia Cavalry, the older brother of my two comrades, and messmates, Carter and John Page. "Bob" was one of the "true blues" who had followed Stuart's feather from the start, and was going to follow it to the bitter end. I remember how, at the very first, he rode off to the war, from his home, "Locust Grove," in Cumberland County, Virginia, on his horse, "Goliath," with his company, the Cumberland Troop. He had stuck to the front, been always up, and ever at his post, all the way through those three long, terrible years. He had deserved, and won his Lieutenancy, and commanded his regiment the last days of the war. He made an enviable record as a soldier for courage, faithfulness, and honor. None better! At Appomattox he was surrendered. And having been forced to cease making war on mankind with the saber, he mended his grip, and continued to make war, with a far deadlier weapon of destruction, the spatula.

All this was very pleasant, but it was very short. Time was up; ten minutes were out! We caught sight of General Stuart cantering across the field toward our guns, the bugle rang, and we tumbled out from amidst the cavalry, in short order, and took our posts around our respective guns.

"Jeb" Stuart Assigns "A Little Job"

Stuart was in front of the column of guns talking to Captain McCarthy; next moment we moved. That is, the "Left Section" moved, the two twelve-pounder brass "Napoleons," the "Right Section" had two ten-pounder "Parrott" guns and stayed still. We did not rejoin them for several days. It was our "Napoleons" that moved off, we took note of that! Also, we took very scant gun detachments,—all our men, but just enough to work the guns, stayed behind,—we took note of *that* too! These two circumstances meant *business* to old artillerymen. We *remarked* as much, as we trotted beside the guns. "The little job" that General Stuart had alluded to, with his bland and seductive smile, and the merry twinkle of his eye, was, plainly, a very *warm* little job; however, away we went, "J. E. B." Stuart riding in front of the guns, with the Captain,—apparently enjoying himself; *we reserved our opinion* as to the enjoyableness of the occasion, till we should *see more* and be better able to judge. Two guns of "Callaway's" and two of "Carlton's" Batteries of our Battalion,—which had come up while we were disporting with our cavalry friends, back there,—had pulled in behind our two.

The six guns followed the road which turned around the farmhouse, and ran on down toward the back of the farm. There were pine woods about, in different directions, the fields lying between. We saw nothing as yet, and wondered where we were going. We soon found out! About half a mile from the house, the farm road, which here ran along with pine woods on the left and a stretch of open field on the right, turned out toward the open ground. As we passed out from behind that point of woods, we saw "the elephant!" There, about six hundred yards from us were the Federals, seeming to cover the fields. There were lines of infantry, batteries, wagons, ambulances, ordnance trains massed all across the open ground. This was part of Warren's Corps, which had been pushing for the Spottsylvania line. They thought they had left the "Army of Northern Virginia" back yonder at the "Wilderness," and had nothing before them but cavalry, and they were halted, now, resting or eating, intending afterwards to advance, and occupy the line, which was back up behind us, where we had left the cavalry and our other guns. That line, so coveted, so important to them, that they had been marching, and fighting to gain, was not a mile off, in sight, in reach, *secure now*, as they thought. That thought was not only a *delusion*, it was a *snare*. They were never to reach it! and the "snare," I will explain very soon.

As we thus suddenly came upon that sight, we stopped to look at the spectacle. It looked very blue, and I dare say, we looked a shade "blue" ourselves; for we could not see a Confederate anywhere, and we supposed we had no support whatever, though we were better

From the Rapidan to Richmond and the Spottsylvania Campaign

off in this particular than we knew. And the idea of pitching into that host, with six unsupported guns, was not calming to the mind. Coming out from cover of the pines, back of a slight ridge that ran through the field, with a few sassafras bushes on it, we were not seen, and the Federals were in blissful ignorance of what was about to follow. We pulled diagonally across the field to a point, just back of the low ridge, and quietly went into position and unlimbered the guns. We pushed them, by hand, up so that the muzzles just looked clear over the ridge, which thus acted as a low work in our front, and proved a great protection. The field had been freshly plowed for corn, the wheels sunk into it, and the minute we tried to move the guns, by hand, with our small force, we saw what it was going to be, in action, with the sun blazing down.

When all was ready,—guns pointed, limber, and caisson chests opened,—General Stuart said, waving his hand toward that swarming field of Federals, "Boys, I want you to knock that all to pieces for me. So go to work." And this was the last time we ever saw the superb hero. He rode, right from our guns, to his death at "Yellow Tavern" a day or two after. We have always remembered with the deepest interest, that the very last thing that glorious soldier, "J. E. B." Stuart, did in the Army of Northern Virginia was to put our guns into position, and give us orders; which *we obeyed*, to his entire satisfaction, I know, if he had seen it.

The minute General Stuart had given his order, and turned to ride away, Captain McCarthy, sitting on his horse, where he sat during the whole fight, looking as cool as the sun would let him, and far more unconcerned than if he had been going to dinner, sung out, "Section — — commence firing." It was ours, the Fourth gun's turn to open the ball. We were all waiting around the guns for the word.

The group, as it stood, is before my mind as vividly as then. Dan McCarthy, Sergt. Ned Stine, acting gunner (vice Tony Dibrell absent, sick, for some time past, who came tearing back, *still sick*, the moment he heard we were on the warpath) Ben Lambert, No. 1; Joe Bowen, No. 2; Beau Barnes, No. 3; W. M. Dame, No. 4; Bill Hardy, No. 5; Charlie Pleasants, No. 6; Sam Vaden, No. 7; Watt Dibbrell, No. 8! The three drivers of the limber, six yards back of the gun, dismounted, and holding their horses. Ellis, the lead driver, had scooped out the loose dirt, with his hands, and lay down, on his back, in the shallow hole, holding the reins with his upstretched hands.

From the Rapidan to Richmond and the Spottsylvania Campaign

The third gun was just to our right, the cannoneers grouped around the guns, each man at his post. Travis Moncure, Sergeant, known and loved and honored among us as "Monkey," always brave and true and smiling, even under fire, Harry Townsend, gunner; Cary Eggleston, No. 1; Pres Ellyson, No. 2; ———— Denman, No. 3; Charlie Kinsolving, No. 4; Charlie Harrington, No. 5; ————, No. 6; ————, No. 7; ————, No. 8; Captain McCarthy sitting his horse, just behind, and between the two guns. The other guns were a little to our left.

All was ready; guns loaded and pointed, carefully, every man at his post,—feeling right solemn too,—and a dead stillness reigned. The Captain's steady voice rang out! As an echo to it, Dan McCarthy sung out "Fourth detachment commence firing, fire!" I gave the lanyard a jerk. A lurid spout of flame about ten feet long shot from the mouth of the old "Napoleon," then, in the dead silence, a ringing, crashing roar, that sounded like the heavens were falling, and rolled a wrathful thunder far over the fields and echoing woods. Then became distinct, a savage, venomous scream, along the track of the shell. This grew fainter,—died on our ear! We eagerly watched! Suddenly, right over the heads of the enemy, a flash of fire, a puff of snow-white smoke, which hung like a little cloud! We gave a yell of delight; our shell had gone right into the midst of the Federals, and burst beautifully. The ball was open!

The instant our gun fired we could hear old Moncure sing out, "Third detachment, commence firing, fire!" and the Third piece rang out. The guns on the left joined in, lustily, and in a moment, those six guns were steadily roaring, and hurling a storm of shell upon the enemy.

And now the fun began, and soon "grew fast and furious." Over in the Federal lines, taken by surprise, all was confusion, worse confounded. We could see men running wildly about, teamsters, jumping into the saddle, and frantically lashing their horses,—wagons, ambulances, ordnance carts, battery forges, tearing furiously, in every direction. Several vehicles upset, and many teams, maddened by the lash, and the confusion, and bursting shells, dashing away uncontrollable. We saw *one* wagon, flying like the wind, strike a stump, and thrown, team and all, a perfect wreck, on top of a low rail fence, crushing it down, and rolling over it.

This was the only time I ever saw a big army wagon, and team, thrown over a fence.

From the Rapidan to Richmond and the Spottsylvania Campaign

All that lively time they were having over among the enemy was very amusing to us; we were highly delighted, and enjoyed it very much. Laughter, and jocular remarks on the scene were heard all about, as we worked the gun, and we did our best to keep up the show.

Meanwhile, we were not deceived for a moment. Wild and furious as was the confusion, and running, over the way, we knew, well, it was the wagoners and "bomb-proof" people, who were doing the running, and stirring up the confusion. We knew they were not *all* running away. We had seen a good deal of artillery in that field, and we knew that we should soon hear from them. And we were not mistaken!

In a few minutes the sound of our guns was suddenly varied by a sharp, venomous screech, clap of thunder, right over our heads, followed by a ripping, tearing, splitting crash, that filled the air; a regular blood freezer. We knew *that sound*! It was a bursting Parrott shell from a Federal gun! And they had the range.

The enemy had run out about eighteen, or twenty guns, and they let in, mad as hornets. Another shell, and another, and another, came screaming over us. Then they began to *swarm*; the air seemed full of them,—bursting shells, jagged fragments, balls out of case-shot,—it sounded like a thousand devils, shrieking in the air all about us. Then, the roaring of our guns, the heavy smoke, the sulphurous smell, the shaking of the ground under the thunder of the guns,—it was a fit place for *devils* to shriek in.

And how *hot* it was! Twenty guns, in full fire, can make it hot at the foot of the North Pole, and this was *not* the North Pole! quite the reverse. In addition to the battle heat, the sun was pouring down, hot as blazes; and the labor of working a rapidly firing "Napoleon" gun, with four men, in deeply plowed ground, and the strong excitement of battle—altogether, it was the hottest place I ever saw, or hope I shall *ever* see, in this world, or in the world to come. It nearly melted the marrow in our bones!

A persimmon sapling stood near our gun. It was trimmed, and chipped down, twig by twig, and limb by limb, by pieces of shell, until it was a lot of *scraps scattered over the ground*. Sam Vaden, as he passed me, with a shell, said "Dame, just look back over this field behind us. A mosquito couldn't fly across that field without getting hit." It looked so! The dirt was being knocked up, wherever you looked, literally, by *shower* of balls, and shell fragments. It had the appearance of hail striking on the surface of water, only it wasn't cold.

Well! for three mortal hours this battle raged. They hammered us, and we hammered them. Occasionally, we saw a Federal caisson blown up, which refreshed us, and several of their guns ceased firing—disabled or cannoneers cleared out, we thought—and *this* refreshed us. We wished they would *all* blow up, and stop shooting.

After we had been under fire sometime, with nobody hurt as yet, a case-shot burst in front of us, and Hardy, who had just brought up a shell, and was standing right by me, said, in his usual deliberate way, "Dame, I'm hit, and hit very hard, I am afraid." "Where are you hit?" I asked. He said, "I'm shot through the thigh, and the leg is numbed." I fired the gun, and jumped down to see what I could do for him. I found the place, and it looked ugly. There was a clean-cut hole right through his pants, to the thickest part of the thigh. I put my finger into the hole, and tore away the cloth to get at the wound, and found to my great, and his *greater* delight, that the ball had struck, and glanced. It had made a long black bruise and the pain was much greater than if it had gone through the leg. It had struck the great mass of muscle on the outer thigh, and the leg was, for the time, paralyzed and stiff as a poker. He was completely disabled. I said, "Bill, you must get right away from here." "But I *can't* walk a step." "Well crawl off on your hands and your good foot, not a man could leave the gun, to help you, and go out to the side so as to get soonest from under fire." So the poor fellow hobbled off, as best he could, all alone, amidst the laughter of the fellows at his novel locomotion. We could see the bullets knocking up the dirt all around him, as he went slowly "hopping the clods" across the plowed fields. But he got off all right. Shortly after Hardy was struck, Charley Pleasants, of Richmond No. ———, at the Third gun, was shot through the thigh. A long and tedious wound which kept him disabled some months. Bill Hardy was back to duty in a day or so. One of the horses, the off horse of the wheel team of our limber, was hit, also. A piece of shell went into his head, between the right eye and ear, cutting the brow band of the bridle. The old horse, a character in the Battery, didn't seem to mind it; and he wore that piece of shell, in his head, until the end of the war.

And, strange as it seemed, these were all our casualties, under that hot fire; one man, seriously, and one slightly wounded and a horse slightly hurt.

Wounding of Robert Fulton Moore

No! I forgot! There was one other casualty,—Robert Fulton Moore was mortally wounded, *in the hat brim*. And this gave rise to a most amusing scene. Robert Fulton was a driver to the limber of the third gun. He was a large, soft, man, and was, by no means, characterized by soldierly bearing, or warlike sentiments. On the contrary, he was something of a "butt," and was always desperately unhappy under fire. He could dodge lower off the back of a horse at sound of a shell, than any man living. His miraculous feats, in this performance, afforded much diversion, whenever the guns went under fire, to us all, except his Sergeant, Moncure, who was very much ashamed of it. Still, in a general, feeble sort of way Robert Fulton had managed to keep up without any flagrant act of flinching from his post. On this occasion he had stood up better than usual. He stood holding his horses, and we noticed, with pleasure, that he was behaving very well under fire. But, it seems, his courage was only "hanging by the eyelids" so to speak.

Presently a piece of shell came whizzing very close to his head. It cut away part of his hat brim, and alas! this was too much! Poor Robert Fulton went all to pieces, instantly. Completely demoralized, panic-stricken and frantic with terror, he dropped his reins, and struck out wildly. It seems, he had seen Ellis, our lead driver, scooping out the hole that has been referred to, and as this was the only hole of any kind in reach, he instinctively struck for it. Ellis was lying down in it, flat on his back, with his arms stretched upward, holding his horses. Robert Fulton rounded the limber, and threw himself down with all his weight, right upon, and completely covering up, Ellis, and stuck his face in the dirt over Ellis' shoulder, effectually pinning him down. Ellis was a fiery, ugly-tempered fellow, but as brave as Julius Cæsar, and of all men in the battery he had the greatest contempt for Moore, and especially for his present conduct. Ellis, upon finding Moore on top of him, was in a perfect blaze of fury. The breath was nearly knocked out of him by Moore's weight, and he was mashed into the narrow hole, and embarrassed by the reins of his horses. He tried to throw Moore off, and couldn't. Then he broke loose! He yelled, and swore, and bit, and pulled Moore's hair, and socked his spurs into him, with both feet. He would have broken a blood vessel if McCarthy, assisted by Moncure, who had come to look after his driver, had not pulled Moore off, and taken him back to his post.

Our attention was drawn to this scene by the noise. The terrific combat going on in that hole, the sight of Ellis' legs and arms, tossing wildly in the air, Moore not moving a muscle, but lying still, on top, the dust kicked up by the fray,—it was more than flesh and blood could stand, even under such a fire, and we could hardly work the guns for laughing. After the fight, when Moore had time to look into his injuries, he found that Ellis had nearly skinned him with his spurs. Some days after, we heard Robert Fulton exhibiting his torn hat brim to some passing acquaintance from his own neighborhood, as a trophy of his prowess in this fight. No doubt he preserves it as a sacred relic yet.

A Useful Discovery

In this fight, necessity, the mother of invention, put us up to a device that served us well here, and that we made fullest use of, in every fight we had afterwards. When we had kept up that rapid fire, with a scant gun detachment, in plowed ground, and under a hot sun, for an hour, we were nearly exhausted. After Hardy was wounded, and left us, it was still worse. The hardest labor, and what took most time, was running up the guns from the recoil. We had stopped a moment to rest, and let the gun cool a little, and were discussing the difficulties, when the idea occurred to us. There was an old rail fence near by. Somebody said "let's get some rails and chock the wheels to keep them from running back." This struck us all as good, and in an instant we had piled up rails behind the wheels as high as the trail would allow. The effect was, that when the gun fired it simply jerked back against this rail pile, and rested in its place, and so we were saved all the time and labor of running up. We found that we could fire three or four times as rapidly, in this way. So that a chocked gun was equal to four in a fight. We found this simple device of immense service! We were told by the knowing ones that we ran the greatest possible danger. The ordnance people said that if a gun was not allowed to recoil it would certainly burst. But we didn't mind! A device that saved so much labor, and enabled us to deliver such an extraordinarily effective fire on the battlefield, we were bound to try. We found it acted beautifully. We then *knew* the guns *wouldn't* burst for we had tried it.

We used it afterward in every fight. The instant we were ordered into position, two or three cannoneers would rush off and get rails, or a log or two, to chock the guns. And on two or three very desperate emergencies, during this campaign, this device enabled us to render very important service. It made a battery equal to a battalion, and a good many other batteries took it up, and used it. I believe it added greatly to the effectiveness of our artillery in the close-range fighting of this campaign.

Well! even with this relief, the labor of working our guns in this furious and prolonged fight was fearful! At last the welcome order, "Section cease firing" was given. We limbered up, and drew the guns a short distance to the side, out of the line of fire, and utterly exhausted, we cannoneers, threw ourselves right down on the plowed ground beside the guns, and slept like the dead.

In the meantime, while we had been fighting out in that field, events were taking place near us, of which we, absorbed in the work before us and deafened by the roar of our guns, had taken little notice at the time. As had been described, there was a body of woods some distance off to our right, and another, to our left. When we went into position we had not seen any of our troops, and did not know of the presence of any, near us. We thought we were without support, but as I intimated some time back, we were better off than we knew.

Barksdale's Mississippi Creeper

It seems, that before we came on the ground, Barksdale's Mississippi Brigade, which had been marching behind us, had filed off the road, and while we were up on the hill with the cavalry, had quietly, and silently passed into that body of woods to our right, unseen by the enemy. Along the front edge of that wood ran an old rail fence, covered all over with the luxuriant vine known as "Virginia Creeper." Wide open fields extending in front. Soon, the ground behind that fence was covered with another sort of "creeper," not as good a "runner" as that on the fence, nor as "green," but just as tough of fibre, and as hard to "hold on" when it had once fixed itself,—the "*Mississippi* Creeper." Silently, as ghosts, the Brigade glided in behind that fence, and lay low, and waited. Right here, was where the Federals' idea of *quietly* occupying the Spottsylvania line was going to prove a snare. They had not the dimmest suspicion that we were ahead of them, and between them and that line. They came on, with guileless confidence, and walked right into trouble. Presently, a line of battle with columns of troops behind came marching across the fields upon the concealed Mississippians. Nearer and nearer they came, unsuspecting any danger, till they got nearly up to the fence. One man had actually thrown his leg over the rail to mount. Suddenly! as lightning out of a clear sky, a blinding sheet of flame flashed into their very faces. Then, after one volley, swiftly came the dreadful, venomous roll of musketry, the

From the Rapidan to Richmond and the Spottsylvania Campaign

Mississippians loading and firing "at will," every man as fast as he could. It was just as if "the angel of death spread his wings to the blast and breathed in the face of the foe as he passed."

That withering fire tore the ranks of that Division to pieces. It didn't take those fellows half a second to decide what to do. With yells of dismay, they charged back, out of that hornet's nest, as if the devil was after them. In headlong rout, they rushed wildly back across the fields, and disappeared in the woods beyond.

They left four hundred and two of their number in front of that fence, and before the fugitives got out of range, their General of Division, General Robinson, was seriously wounded.

Some of our men went out among the Federal wounded to do what they could for their relief. An officer of a Mississippi Regiment came upon a Federal Colonel who lay to all appearance mortally wounded, and gave him a drink of water, and did what else he could for his comfort. The Federal took out a fine gold watch, and said, "Here is a watch that I value very highly. You have been very kind to me, and I would like you to have it, as I am going to die. If I should get over this, and send to you for it you will let me have it, if not, I want you to keep it. But," he said sadly, "my wound is mortal, I am obliged to die." The Mississippian left him, and went back to his post, supposing him dead.

Many years after the war, the Mississippi officer was in Baltimore at Barnum's Hotel. One day, he got into casual talk with a gentleman, at dinner, and, as he seemed to be a good fellow, they smoked their cigars together after dinner, and continued their conversation. By and by they got on the war. It came out, that both of them had served, and on opposite sides. Finally, in telling some particular incidents of his experience, the Federal soldier described this very fight, his being, as he thought mortally wounded, the kindness shown him by a Confederate officer, and his gift to him, of his watch. The Southern man said, "What is your name?" "Col. — — — —, of Robinson's Division," he replied. "Can you be the man? Have I struck you at last?" cried the ex-Confederate. "*I've* got your watch, and here it is, with your name engraved in it."

Kershaw's South Carolina "Rice Birds"

It was a singular incident, that these two should meet again so! The meeting was most cordial; the Federal was delighted to get his watch again, made doubly valuable by so strange a history.

From the Rapidan to Richmond and the Spottsylvania Campaign

While this bloody episode was enacting by the Mississippi Brigade, in the woods to our right, an almost exactly similar scene was going on, in the woods to our left. A portion of Kershaw's South Carolina Brigade was unwittingly stumbled upon by "Griffin's" Division in the pines. Another complete ambuscade! The South Carolinians suddenly sprang up before the Federals, let them have it, broke and routed them, and killed, and wounded eighty-seven of them. Our loss was one man. Things were so sudden, so close here, that one of Kershaw's men killed a Federal soldier, and wounded another with an axe he happened to have in his hand.

These first efforts of "Warren's" Corps that had gotten up near the Spottsylvania line, "just in time to be too late," are thus described by Swinton, the admirable historian of the "Army of the Potomac." (Swinton's "Army of the Potomac," p. 443):

"Finally," he says, "the column (Warren's) emerged from the woods into a clearing, two miles north of Spottsylvania Court House. Forming in line, Robinson's Division advanced over the plain. Thus far, only Stuart's dismounted troops had been encountered, and no other opposition was anticipated; but when half way across the field, and on the point of rising the crest, the troops were met by a savage musketry fire from infantry. Owing to their severe experience in the Wilderness, and the night march, without rest, the men were in an excited, and almost frightened, condition, and the tendency to *stampede* was so great that General Warren had been compelled to go in front of the leading Brigade. When, therefore, they received a fire in front, from the redoubtable foe they had left in the Wilderness, the line wavered, and fell back in some confusion. General Robinson was at the same time severely wounded, which left the troops without their commander at a critical moment, and they were with some difficulty rallied and reformed in the woods back of the open plain. Griffin's Division, which advanced on the right of Robinson, soon afterward received the same fire with a like result."

It seems then, that it was Robinson's Division that the little Mississippi Brigade sent to the right about, and it was Griffin's Division, who scared themselves nearly into fits, by flushing Kershaw's "rice-birds," in the pines. It was a little hard on these "excited and almost frightened" men of Warren's. The memory of the fearful shaking up they had got, day before yesterday, was so fresh in their minds that "General Warren himself, the *Corps Commander*, had to go in front of the leading Brigade" to quiet their nerves, even when they thought they were advancing upon a few dismounted troops. They thought,—a little comfort in this,—that, at least, all those terrible fellows of the Army of Northern Virginia were far behind them. And—to meet them *here*, still, in front! It must be confessed it was hard! It was a very sad surprise.

It is said that General Grant's strained relations with General Warren came of Warren's conduct of this move, to seize the Spottsylvania line. He found great fault with his failure. But, perhaps he was a little hard on Warren. What could Warren do? His men were demoralized, "excited, almost frightened, tending to stampede, needing the Corps General to go in front," and stopping to dine, instead of pushing on to seize the line. They had to meet men who were not *particularly excited*, were not *at all frightened* and had not *the least tendency to stampede*; in fact, were in the best of spirits, perfectly confident of victory, and did not need *a corporal to go in front of them*, gaunt, hungry, cool fellows, who never counted noses—in a fight!

It was too much to expect Warren, with men like his, to go anywhere, or take anything, when men like these others were in the way. Grant was too hard on Warren! If it took a *Corps Commander*, going in front, to encourage them along to advance upon *a few troopers*. I hardly think that Generals Grant and Meade, and President Lincoln, and Secretary Stanton, *all together*,—going in front, could have got them up, *if they had known who was actually ahead*.

However that may be, the object of our rapid all-night march, and of our venturesome stand, out here, in front of the Spottsylvania line, was accomplished! The stir up we gave them with that long artillery fire, and the savage and bloody repulses of two of their divisions made them more nervous than they were before. They spent some time considering who it could be in their front, and considering what to do. Later on, two more Divisions advanced, and our two Brigades and our guns retired.

Our work was done! While we had been out in front amusing the enemy, and keeping them easy, the Brigades of Longstreet's Corps had been rapidly coming up, and taking position on the all-important line. We now had a *sure enough line of battle* holding it. And night was falling; the enemy out in front had stopped, and gone to intrenching, instead of pushing on. We knew that during that night our people, Ewell and Hill, would be up. All were safe! We slept the sleep of the weary. So ended the 8th of May. It was a pretty full day for us!

I don't remember anything at all about the early morning of the next day, the 9th. We were dreadfully tired, and I suppose we slept late, and then lounged about, with nothing to do, yet, in a listless, stupid state. Everything was quiet around us, and nothing to attract attention, or fix it in mind. About mid-day, I recollect noticing bodies of troops, a regiment, a brigade, or two, moving about, here and there, in various directions. We heard that Ewell's and Hill's Corps had come up, and these troops we saw, were taking their way leisurely, along, to the various position on the line of battle.

In the afternoon, about four or five o'clock, our guns, the "Napoleon" Section, moved off to take our destined position on the line. We followed a farm road, off toward the left, and presently came down into quite a decided hollow, through which ran a little stream of water. Here we halted! The ground before us rose into a low short hill. Along the ridge of that hill ran the proposed line of battle, and there was the position for which we were making. There was quite a lively picket fire going on, in different directions, and right over the hill, behind which we were, an occasional shell could be heard screeching about, here and there. Several passed over us, high above our heads, and away to the rear. Federal Artillery lazily feeling about to provoke a reply, and find out where somebody was. They felt lonesome, perhaps! It was a calm, sweet sunlit May evening.

Feeling Pulses

In order not to expose us longer than necessary to this fire of the pickets, Lieutenant Anderson, commanding this "Section," went up on the hill, to select *exact* position for the guns, so that they might be promptly placed, when we went up. While he was up there reconnoitering, we lay down on the ground, and waited, and talked. The bullets dropped over, near, and among us, now and then, and we knew, that the moment we went up a few steps, on the hill, we would be a mark for sharp-shooters, a particularly unpleasant situation for artillery. But we tried to forget all this, and be as happy and *seem* as careless as we could. And we would have gotten along very well if let alone. But, there was a dreadful, dirty, snuffy, spectacled old Irishman, named Robert Close, a driver, who took this interval to amuse himself. He would ask us "how we felt," and he came around to most of us, young fellows, and asked us to let him feel our pulse, and see if we were at all excited, or scared; and he would put his hand on our hearts, to see if they were beating regularly enough. And he would call out the result of his investigation in each case,—the other fellows all sitting around, and eagerly waiting his report. Nobody can tell what a dreadful trial this simple thing was! When just going under fire—and indeed *already* under some fire—to have your heart and your pulse felt, and reported on to a waiting crowd of comrades! But, all of us youngsters had to undergo it! That cruel, old scoundrel went round to every one of the youngsters. It was an unspeakable humiliation for a *cannoneer* to be thus fingered by *a driver*, but what could we do? Not a thing!

We would *have liked* to knock the old rascal's head off, but, not one of us would have dared to object to that pulse feeling, and we in turn meekly held out our wrists, and *tried* to look happy and amused—and made a dismal failure of it. Old Close was as brave, himself, as a lion. *He* had as soon go in a fight as not; a little sooner! When balls swarmed around, he didn't care a bit. He was in a position to do this thing. But it was suffering to us. Each man waited, with anxious heart, for his turn to come, for old Close to "pass upon his condition." Those whom he approved, were pleased to death, and those whom he didn't, hated him from that time.

I honestly believe that old Irishman gave me the worst scare I had in that campaign, and I am sure that a compliment, on the field, from General Longstreet himself, would not have pleased me more, than that snuffy old fellow's verdict, after feeling my pulse that I "would do all right." It was quite a curious scene altogether!

Where the Fight Was Hottest

In a few minutes Lieutenant Anderson came down and ordered us forward. He told us "the sharp-shooters were making it a little warm" up there. When the guns got to the top of the rise, they must go at a trot to their positions, the sooner to get the horses from under fire. Twenty or thirty steps brought us to the top of the sharp little ascent. Here we found a few of our sharp-shooters exchanging compliments with the enemy, and the balls were knocking up the dirt, and whistling around. I was interested in watching one of our fellows. He was squatting down, holding his rifle ready. A Federal sharp-shooter, whom we could not see, was cracking at him. Three times a ball struck right by him, and came whizzing by us. He kept still, and patiently bided his time. Suddenly, he threw up his rifle and fired, and then exclaimed "Well! I got *you* anyhow." The balls stopped coming. This man said that the concealed Federal sharp-shooter had been shooting at him for some time and he had been waiting for him. At last, catching sight of a head rising from behind a bush, he got his chance, as we saw, and dropped his man. Our guns were placed in their position, selected for them on the line, and the horses sent back to the rear.

Our position here was right on the infantry line of battle. That is, on that line the infantry afterwards took. For when we got on the spot, there was no infantry there,—nothing except the sharp-shooters, already referred to. The line was traced by a continuous pile of dirt thrown up, I don't know by whom, before we got on the ground. I suppose the engineers had it done as a guide to the troops, in taking position.

The position our guns now took, grew to be very familiar ground to us, and remains very memorable. On this spot we stayed, and fought our part in the Spottsylvania battles. On this spot we saw many bloody sights, and witnessed many heroic scenes, and had many thrilling experiences. The incidents of those days spent there, in nearly all their details, are indelibly impressed on my memory, and are as fresh as if they happened yesterday.

We stood on a low ridge which rose gradually to the right. To the left, after running level for fifty yards, the ground fell rapidly away, until it sank down into the valley of a little brook, one hundred and fifty yards from us. Off to the left, in front, stretched a large body of woods. To the right, in front, stood a body of thick pines coming up to within two or three hundred yards of us, its edge running along to the right about that distance parallel with our line. Directly in front of us, the ground,—cleared fields about three or four hundred yards wide,—sloped gently away down to a stream, and beyond, sloped gently upward to the top of the hill, on which stood a farmhouse, and buildings. That hill was considerably higher than our position, and commanded it. That hill-top was about one-half to three-quarters of a mile from us.

All along our front, in the bottom, ran a little stream; the ground, on either side, in our immediate front, was swampy, and thickly covered with low swamp growth. That soft ground saved us a good many hard knocks we had plenty as it was! Behind us, our cleared ground ran back, very gently sloping, almost level, some thirty or forty yards, and then, the hill fell sharply down, some twenty yards to the little brook, which ran along the hollow! This sharp bank, facing away from the enemy, and this stream, protected by it, and so near us, proved a great comfort to us. It also was of great service as a covered way, by which troops and supplies (*ammunition*, while there, it did not seem to be considered necessary for us to have any other supplies) were able to approach the line. Once it proved of vital use as a cover behind which a broken Brigade was able to rally, and save the line.

Exactly back of us, forty yards off, and covering that steep bank at this one point, stood a body of large, tall trees,—pines and others,—occupying half an acre. And in that wood, under the bank, some of the fellows dug holes, and in them they built fires which, by one or another, were kept up all the time. At these fires,—quite effectually protected from shot and shell and bullets, though within forty yards of the line of battle, a fellow could cook anything he happened, by accident, to have, or slip back from the works, now and then, when not engaged at the guns, warm himself and stand up straight, and stretch his legs and back, without the imminent risk of being bored by a sharp-shooter; which makes a stretch unsatisfactory.

Just at the point where we were posted, the line left the ridge, and dipping a little, on the front face of the slope, ran along about parallel with the ridge. My gun, "Number Four," stood exactly at the point where the line declined in front of the ridge, and so, was exactly in the infantry line. The "3d gun" was some ten yards to our left, on the ridge seven or eight yards back of the line, and could fire over it to the front. It had its own separate work.

It was about sunset when we got to our position. We unlimbered our guns, and ran them up close to the bank of dirt, about two feet high, which we found there, thinking that in case of a row, that would be some little protection. However, things seemed quiet. We couldn't see any enemy from where we stood, didn't know whether any force was near us. And after we placed our guns, we strolled around, and looked about us, and were disposing ourselves for a quiet night, and a good sleep, which we needed badly.

Just then somebody, I think it was Lieutenant Anderson, who had walked to the left, some distance, where he could see around the point of pine woods to our right, up on the hill, came back with some news very interesting to us, if not to our advantage. He said that, just beyond these woods up on the hill, not over five or six hundred yards from us, there was a lot of Federal artillery. He saw them plainly. They were in position. He counted twelve guns, and was sure there were others, farther around, which he could not see for the woods. At least six of those, in sight, he was certain were twenty-pounder Parrotts. These guns, he said, commanded our position, and while the enemy had not yet seen us, for the treetops between, they soon would; and *anyhow*, the moment we fired a shot, and disclosed our position, we would catch it. There were enough heavy guns bearing down on us to sweep us off the face of the earth, unless we were protected. If daylight found us unfortified we couldn't stay there, so we had better go to throwing dirt.

Against Heavy Odds at "Fort Dodge"

Here was nice news! Our two Napoleons, right under the muzzles of twelve or more rifled cannon, and six twenty-pounder Parrotts, and with no works! This was pleasant advice to tired and sleepy men, who wanted to go to bed. But such were the facts, and as we never had left a position under fire, and had come to stay, and were *certainly going* to stay, we *went* to throwing dirt.

We went to work, to raise and thicken the little bank already there, in front of our gun, and to build a short "traverse" to the right, for protection from enfilade fire. We worked all night, six of us, and by morning we had a slight and rough artillery work, with an embrasure for the gun; the whole thing about four feet high, and two and one-half feet thick, at the top. It was the best that could be done by six, tired, and hungry fellows, all young boys, working with two picks and three shovels through a short night. Such as it was, we fought behind it, all through the Spottsylvania battles, and it stood some heavy battering. This gem of engineering skill,—by reason of the pretty constant courtesies we felt it polite to pay to the unceasing attentions of our friends, the enemy, for the next six days, in the shape of shells and bullets, we called "Fort *Dodge*."

Just here, I take occasion to correct a very wrong impression about the field works, the "Army of Northern Virginia" fought behind, in this campaign. All the Federal writers who have written about these battles, speak of our works as "formidable earthworks," "powerful fortifications," "impregnable lines;" such works as *no troops* could be expected *to take*, and any troops could be expected *to hold*.

Now about the parts of the line distant from us, I couldn't speak so certainly, though I am sure they were all very much the same, but about the works all along *our part* of the line I can speak with exactness and certainty. I saw them, I helped, with my own hands, to make them. I fought behind them. I was often on top of them, and both sides of them. I know all about them. I got a good deal of the mud off them on me,—(not for purposes of personal fortification, however).

Our "works" were, a single line of earth, about four feet high, and three to five feet thick. It had no ditch or obstructions in front. It was nothing more than a little heavier line of "rifle pits." There was no physical difficulty in men walking right over that bank! I did it often myself, saw many others do it, and twice, saw a line of Federal troops walk over it, and then saw them walk *back* over it, with the greatest ease, at the rate of forty miles an hour; *i. e.*, except those whom we had persuaded to stay with us, and those whom the angels were carrying to Abraham's bosom, at a still swifter rate. Works they could go over like that couldn't have been much obstacle! They couldn't have made better time on a dead level.

"Sticky" Mud and Yet More "Sticky" Men

Such were our works *actually*! And still, they seemed to "loom largely" to the people in front. I wonder what could have given them such an exaggerated idea of the strength of those modest little works? I wonder if it could have been the *men* behind them? There were not a great many of these men. It was a very thin gray line along there, back of a thin, red line of clay. But these lines stuck together very hard, and were very hard indeed to separate. The red clay was "sticky" and the men were just as "sticky." And, as the two lines stuck together so closely, it made the whole very strong indeed. Certainly, it seems they gave to those who tried to force them apart, an impression of great strength!

Yes, it must have been the *men*. A story in point, comes to my aid here. A handsome, well-dressed lady sweeps with a great air, past two street boys. They are much struck. "My eye, Jim, but ain't that a stunning dress?" Says Jim, with a superior air, "Oh get out, Bill, the dress ain't no great shakes; it's the *woman* in it that makes it so 'killing.'" That was the way with our Spottsylvania earthworks. The works "wa'n't no great shakes." It was the *men* in 'em, that made them so "killing."

The men behind those works, such as they were, had perfect confidence in their own ability to hold them. And this happy combination of "faith" and "works" proved as strong against the world and the flesh, here, as it does against the devil. It was perfectly effectual! It withstood all assaults!

From the Rapidan to Richmond and the Spottsylvania Campaign

This day, May 10th, to whose dawn we have now come, broke dark, and lowering, very typical of the heavy cloud of war that was impending, and soon burst upon us, in a fierce tempest, that was going to thunder, and howl, and beat upon us, all day, and for days to come. This day was to be an eventful, and memorable day to us,—crowded full of incident.

Some time during the night, while we were working like beavers on "Fort Dodge," infantry had come in, on the line. Soon as they got there they set in to do what we were doing, to raise, and thicken the line against the coming of day, and the equally certain coming of battle. When the day came they also, were ready.

Gregg's Texans to the Front

We had been too busy to think about them, at the time, but when we had gotten done,—and had a little time to look about us, and day had broken, and the fighting time, as we knew, was drawing near,—we took an interest in that infantry. Artillerymen are always concerned in their "supports," in a fight, and we wanted to know who these fellows were, on whom we had to depend, as battle comrades, in the approaching struggle. Our minds were quickly made perfectly easy on that score. We found we had alongside of us "Gregg's" Texas Brigade,—the gallant, dashing, stubborn fellows who had, as they jocularly said, "put General Lee under arrest and sent him to the rear," and then, had so brilliantly, and effectually, stopped Hancock's assault on Hill's right, at the Wilderness. Better fellows to have at your back, in a fight, couldn't be found! We knew *that part* of the line was safe! We mingled together, and chatted, and got acquainted, and swapped yarns about our several adventures. We told them how particularly glad we were to have *them* there, and our personal relations soon grew as cordial as possible.

Our service together on this spot, and our esteem of one another's conduct in battle, made the Texans and the "Howitzers" ardent mutual admirers, and fast friends, to the end. Never afterwards did we pass each other, during the campaign, without hearty cheers, each, for the other, and friendly greetings and complimentary references to the "Spottsylvania lines." Gregg's Texans! Noble fellows! Better soldiers never trod a battlefield. I saw them fight; I saw their mettle tried, as by fire. They live in my memory as "the bravest of the brave." I hope Texas is growing more like them!

Breakfastless, But "Ready for Customers"

Having got our Fort in shape, and refreshed ourselves a little with a wash, at the stream back of us, and thinking how nice some breakfast would be, if we had it, (which we *didn't*, not a crumb!) we got ready for the business of the day. We sloped the ground downward to the works, so that the guns would run easily; placed the gun, and saw that it could poke its muzzle well over the dirt, and look around comfortably in every direction; got some rails, and chocked her tight, so that she couldn't run back. Then we got a lot of cartridges, and piled them down safely behind the works, and in front of the guns, so that we could do very rapid firing. Lieutenant Anderson called attention to the fact of these pine woods, in front, which came up to within two or three hundred yards, and that the enemy could get up very near us, under cover, before they started to charge, and we would have to put in our work while they were charging across the narrow open ground. "So," he said, "Have plenty of 'canister' by your guns. Break loose some canisters from the powder, so you can double-shot; you'll need it." We cannoneers had already thought of this; the edge of that wood was in canister range, and we had put little else but this short range missile in our pile; only a few case-shots to make it lively for them in the woods before they came out, and to follow them into the woods, when they were broken, and keep them going. We were now all ready and waited for customers. They soon came!

It was still early in the morning, about five or six o'clock, and, as yet, all was quiet in our front; we hadn't even seen a Federal soldier. Suddenly! out of the woods to our right, just about five hundred yards in front, appeared the heads of three heavy blue columns, about fifty yards apart, marching across the open field toward our left. Here was impudence! Infantry trying to cross our front! *That's* the way it seemed to strike our fellows. I don't know whether they knew our guns were there, but we took it for an insult, and it was with a great deal of personal feeling, we instantly jumped to our guns and loaded with case-shot. Lieutenant Anderson said, "Wait till they get half way across the field. You'll have more chance at them before they can get back into those woods." We waited, and soon they were stretched out to the middle of the field. It was a beautiful mark! Three, heavy well closed up columns, fifty yards apart, on ground gently sloped upward from us, lovely for ricochet shots,— with their flanks to us, and in easy range. Dan McCarthy went up to Ned Stine, our acting gunner, who was very deaf, and yelled in his ear, loud enough for the Federals to hear, "Ned, aim at the nearest column, the ricochet pieces of shell will strike the columns beyond." "All right," he bawled back, with his head on one side, "sighting" the gun. "I've got sight on that column, now. Ain't it time to shoot?" This instant Anderson sung out, "Section commence firing! and get in as many shots as you can before they get away." "Yes," shouted Dan, "Fire!" "Eh?" said Ned, putting his hand up to his ear, "What did you say?" "I said Fire! you deaf old fool—Fire!" the last, in a tone calculated for a mile and a half. This fetched him. Ned threw up his hands (the gunner's signal to fire) and we let drive. All Ned wanted was a start, he was only slow in hearing. He jumped in now, and we kept that gun blazing almost continuously. It was the first time Stine had acted gunner, and he did splendidly here, and until Dibbrell, our gunner, got back.

Our first shot struck right in the nearest column, and burst, and we instantly saw a line opened through all three columns, and a great deal of confusion. The shot from the "Third Piece" struck at another point, and burst, just right for effect. I am sure not a single shot missed in that crowd, and we drove them in just as fast as we could. The columns were pretty badly broken, and in two minutes, they were rapidly crossing back into that woods, out of which they had come, and disappeared. The Texans were greatly pleased with this performance. Having nothing to do, as the enemy was out of effective rifle range, they stood around, and watched us work the guns, and noticed, with keen interest, the effect of our shots upon the blue columns, and they made the welkin ring, when the Federals turned to retire.

Parrott's Reply to Napoleon's Twenty to Two

In a minute or two we received notice of our work from another quarter. That artillery, up there on the hill, beyond the woods, woke up. They got mad at our treatment of their infantry friends, furiously mad. "Boom" went a loud report, over the way, and, the same instant, a savage shriek right over our heads, of a twenty pounder Parrott shell. Another followed, another, and another. They began to rain over. We could detect the sound of different shells, three inch rifle, ten pounder Parrott, and twenty pounder Parrott.

Some fifteen or twenty guns joined in, and they hammered away most savagely. Most fortunately the treetops of that wood, out in our front, came up just high enough to conceal us from the enemy. They could see our smoke, and knew just *about* our position, but they could not *exactly see us*, and correct their aim by the smoke of their shells. So they could not get the *exact* range. And that makes a great difference, in artillery firing, as it does in a great many other things. To know *just about* and to know *exactly*, are two very different things in effect, and in satisfaction to the worker. If those people could have *seen* our two guns, I suppose they could have smashed them both, and killed, or wounded every man of us, and their columns could have moved across our front, in peace, and accomplished this movement they were trying to get across them for, and about which they seemed very anxious. As it was, neither man, nor gun, of ours, was touched, though it was hot as pepper all around there; and our guns stuck there a thorn in their sides, and broke up that movement altogether.

It seems that those columns were a part of Warren's Corps, and were trying to push into an interval between our Corps, and A. P. Hill's Corps, which, under command of General Jubal Early (Hill being very sick) began just on our left, our position being on the left of Longstreet's line, near its junction with Hill's. This infantry was pushing across our front to get into that gap, and make it hot for "Old Jubal" over there in the woods. But, in order to get to that gap, they were forced to pass close to us, and across that open field.

Now, at once, to insult us, and to hurt our friends, was a move that we didn't at all approve, and were not going to stand. And as soon as we discovered the meaning of this move, we were very earnest to stop it.

Well! we had stopped it once, and driven back the Federal columns of attack. It remained to see what they were going to do about it. The Federal artillery thundered at us through the trees. We quietly sat and waited to see.

In about half an hour, (I suppose they thought we were pulverized by the fire their guns had been pouring upon us,) we saw those three infantry columns pouring out of the woods again, at a quick step. We manned the guns, and waited as before, till they reached the middle of the field. Then we began to plow up the columns with shrapnel. This time some of our infantry tried and found it in range for their muskets and they adjusted their rifle sights and took careful aim, with a rest on the top of the works. Soon, the columns faltered, then stopped, then broke, and made good time back to their woods. We could see their officers trying to rally them, but they refused to hear "the voice of the charmer." Soon they disappeared!

Then the artillery began to pour in their shells on us more furiously than ever! The air around us was kept in a blaze, and a roar of bursting shells, and the ground, all about, was furrowed and torn. We quietly sat behind our works, and interchanged our individual observations on what had just taken place, and waited for further developments.

The two rifled pieces of our Battery, and the other rifled guns of our Battalion, "Cabells," had been laced in position, on a hill half a mile back of, and higher, than the low hill on which we were. The plan was for these long range guns to fire over our heads, at the enemy. We suspected that when that Federal infantry next tried to pass us, they would try to make a rush. So Lieutenant Anderson sent back to the other guns, calling attention to this probability, and suggesting that they should be on the lookout, and reinforce our fire, and try, also, to divert the Federal artillery, a little. We thought that with eight or ten rifled guns, added to the fire of ours, and what the infantry could do, we could sicken that Federal infantry of the effort to get by.

Presently we noticed the fire of the Federal guns increase in violence to a marked degree. At this savage outburst, Lieutenant Anderson said, "Boys, get to your guns, that infantry will try to get across under cover of this." We sprang to the guns, and sure enough, in a minute, those blue columns burst out of the woods at a double quick. "Open on them at once men. We can't let them get a start this time," shouted Anderson. Both guns instantly began to drive at the head of their columns.

The sound of our guns started our rifle guns on the hill behind. They opened furiously, and we could hear their shells screeching over our heads, on into this enemy's columns. We did our best, and the Texans did what musket fire they could. The enemy still advanced at a run, but this storm was too much for them. Their columns were torn to pieces, were thrown into hopeless confusion. They had, by this time, gotten half way or more across the field, and they made a gallant effort to keep on, but torn and storm-beaten as they were, they could not stand. The crowd broke and parted. A few ran on across to the farther woods, and were captured by Hill's men. The rest, routed and scattered, ran madly back to the cover they had left. This gave them enough! They gave up the attempt, and tried it no more.

We thought that Hill's Corps "owed us one" for this job. We certainly saved them a lot of trouble by thus protecting their flank. They had to stand a heavy assault by Hancock's Corps, and had very hot work as it was. If these strong columns, that we were taking care of, had gotten into that gap, and taken them at disadvantage, they would have had a hard time, to say the least. Our work left them to deal with Hancock's Corps alone, which they did to their credit, and with entire success, as will appear.

That little scheme of our long-range guns on the hill behind, firing over our heads at the enemy acted very well, for a while. It came to have its very decided inconvenience to *us*, as well as to the enemy. When the Federal infantry had retired, those guns turned their fire on the Federal artillery which was hammering us. They meant to divert their attention, and do us a good turn. They had better have left us to "the ills we had." Their line of fire, at that artillery, was exactly over our position. Very soon their shells got tired travelling over, and began to stop *with us*. Our Confederate shells were often very badly made, the weight in the conical shells not well balanced. And so, very often, instead of going quietly, point foremost, like decent shells, where they were *aimed*, they would get to *tumbling*, that is, going end over end, or "swappin' ends" as the Tar Heels used to describe it, and *then*, there was no telling *where* they would go, except that they would *certainly go wrong*. And, they went very wrong, indeed, on this occasion, in our opinion.

The sound of a tumbling Parrott shell in full flight, is the most horrible noise that ever was heard!—a wild, venomous, fiendish scream, that makes every fellow, in half a mile of it, feel that it is looking for *him particularly*, and *certain* that it's *going to get him*. I believe it would have made Julius Cæsar, himself, "go for a tree," or want to, anyhow!

Well! these blood-curdlers came crashing into us, from the rear, knocking up clouds of dirt, digging great holes, bursting, and raining fragments around us in the field. We were not firing, and had leisure to realize the fix we were in. With the enemy hotly shelling us from the front, and our friends from the rear, obliged to stay by our guns, expecting an infantry assault every minute, we certainly were in a pretty tight fix, "'Tween the devil and the deep sea."

It was the only time I ever saw Lieutenant Anderson excited under fire, but he was excited *now*, and mad too. He said to one of the fellows, "Go back under the hill, get on a horse, ride as hard as you can, and tell those men on the hill, what confounded work they are doing, and if they fire any more shells, here, I will open on them immediately." In a few minutes it was stopped, with many regrets on the part of our friends.

The Narrow Escape of an Entire Company

In the midst of all this, an incident took place that created a great deal of amusement. Along the line, just back of and somewhat protected by the works, the Texans had pitched several of the little "shelter tents" we used to capture from the enemy, and found such a convenience. One of these stood apart. It had a piece of cloth, buttoned on the back, and closing that end up to about eighteen inches from the top, leaving thus, a triangular hole just under the ridge pole. In this little tent sat four men, a captain and three privates, all that were left of a Company in this Texan Brigade. These fellows were playing "Seven-up" and, despite the confusion around, were having a good time. Suddenly, one of the shells from the hill behind, struck, tumbled over once or twice, and stopped, right in the mouth of that tent, the fuse still burning. The game stopped! The players were up, instantly. The next moment, one fellow came diving headforemost out of that triangular hole at the back, followed fast by the other three—the captain last. It only took "one time and one motion" to get out of that. Soon as they could pick themselves up, they, all four, jumped behind a tree that stood there; and then, the fuse went out, and the shell didn't burst. Everybody had seen the shell fall, and were horror stricken at the apparently certain fate of those four men. Now, the absurdity of the scene struck us all, and there were shouts of laughter at their expense. Despite their sudden, hasty retreat through that narrow hole everyone of the scamps had held on to his "hand," and they promptly kicked the shell aside, crawled into the tent again, and continued their little game; interrupted, however, by jokes from all sides. It was very funny! The smoking shell, in front, and those fellows shooting through that hole at the back, and alighting all in a heap, and then the scramble for that tree. As the shell went out, it was a roaring farce. If it hadn't, it would have been a tragedy. The Captain said that these three men were his whole company, and when that lighted shell struck, he thought that his company was "gone up" for good and all.

Such was about the size to which some of the companies of this Texan Brigade was reduced.

From the Rapidan to Richmond and the Spottsylvania Campaign

Well! after we got rid of those shells from the rear we didn't so much mind the artillery fire from the front, which kept up more or less through the morning.

What with the wet, cheerless weather, and the mental discomfort of staying in a place where they were "shooting cannons" at us, and other kind of shooting might soon be expected, two of our men got sick, and went back to the position of our guns on the hill in the rear. The Captain appealed to them to go back, but their health was bad, and they didn't think the place where we were, *a health resort*. So Captain McCarthy called for volunteers to take their places, and instantly John W. Page, and George B. Harrison, of the First Detachment, offered, and came over to us.

Successive Attacks by Federal Infantry

Up to this time we had seen no infantry since their columns had tried to cross our front. No attack had been made on us and all seemed quiet out in front, except that artillery. But, out of our sight, over behind the woods, the enemy was conspiring to break up our quiet in the most decided manner. About ten o'clock we suddenly caught sight of a confused appearance down through the woods on our right front. It quickly defined itself as a line of battle, rapidly advancing. Our pickets fired upon it, then ran back over the works into our line. The Texans sprang into rank, we jumped to our guns, and sent a case-shot tearing down through the woods. Next instant, the Federal line dashed, cheering, out of the edge of the woods, and came charging at us. As they dashed out, they were met by a furious storm of bullets, and cannister, which at two hundred yards tore their ranks. They got about a hundred yards under that fire, then began to falter, then stopped, tried to stand for a moment, then with their battle line shot all to pieces, they turned and broke for the woods in headlong rout. We did our best to help them along, shooting at them with case-shot as long as we could catch any glimpse of them, moving back through the trees. Then that Federal artillery got savage again. We lay low and waited for some more infantry.

Very soon, here they came again! another line charging on, only to meet the same fate; shattered lines, hapless disorder, bloody repulse, and rapid retreat. Several times they tried to reach our lines, and every time failed, then gave it up for the time.

These various assaults took up the time, I should say from ten-thirty to twelve o'clock. When they were over, the field, and wood in front of us displayed a most dreadful scene. The field was thickly strewn with the dead, and wounded. And just along the edge of the wood, where the advancing lines generally first met our full fire, in the several assaults, the dead lay so thick and in such regular order, that it looked to us like a line of battle, lying down. And the poor wounded fellows lying thickly about! It was frightful to see and to hear them. It was a bloody business, their oft-repeated effort to take our line. Their loss was very severe, ours was almost nothing. The Texan Brigade in all their assaults had several wounded, none killed; at our guns not a man was hurt.

One thing that struck me in that fighting was the utter coolness of the Texan infantry. I watched the soldier next to my gun, and can never forget his bearing. The whizzing bullets, the heavy storming columns pouring upon us, the yells and cries of the combatants were enough to excite anybody, but this fellow was just as easy and deliberate as if he had been shooting at a mark. He would drop the butt of his musket on the ground and ram down a cartridge, raise the piece to his hip, put on a cap, cock the hammer, and then, slowly draw the gun up to his eye, and shoot. I really don't think that Texan fired a shot that day until the sight on his gun covered a Federal soldier, and I think it likely he hit a man every time he shot. It was this sort of shooting that made the carnage in front so terrible.

And what a confident lot they were! After one or two of these lines had been repulsed, as the enemy were advancing again, you could hear the men in the line calling one to another, "Say, boys, don't shoot so quick this time! Let them get up closer. Too many of them get away, when you start so soon." Truly they were the unterrified! Our line was so thin; those storming lines of blue as they came storming on seemed *heavy* enough to roll over us like a tidal wave. Yet it never seemed to occur to these fellows that they might be run over. Their only thought was to "let them get up closer next time." Their only concern was that "too many of them were getting away." Good men, they were, to hold a line!

At last, this furious attempt, by Warren and Hancock, to force our position ceased. And as we saw, out in front, the heavy losses of the enemy, and still had every one of our men ready for duty, we thought "*we* could stand this sort of thing, if *they* could, and just as long as they chose to keep on." They lost in dead and wounded about twelve hundred men to about four of ours. Certainly, we could stand it! So we piled some more canister in front of our guns, and watched to see what they would do next.

The long hours crept on until three o'clock, — when the warming up of the Federal artillery fire warned us of another attack. Soon came another stubborn assault by Warren's Corps. Same result. Line after line pushed out from the woods, only to be hurled back, bleeding and torn, leaving on the field large additions to the sad load of dead, and wounded, with which it was already encumbered. They effected nothing! Very little loss to us, heavy loss to them. We were using double shot of canister nearly every time, on masses of men at short range; the infantry fire was rapid and deadly. Our fire soon swept the front clear of the enemy. We piled up more canister, and waited again.

There was now an interval of comparative quiet. We could walk around, and talk, and look about us, a little. Now and then a bullet struck the ground close to us, and presently one of the infantry was struck slightly. It was plain that a concealed sharp-shooter had our range, and we began to watch for him. Soon one of us caught a glimpse of him; he was up a tree some distance out in front, and he would cautiously edge around the trunk and fire, dodging back behind the trunk to load again. One of the Texans went over the works, and stole from stump to stump off toward the left, and for some time was out of our sight. Presently, we saw that sharp-shooter slyly stealing around the tree, and raise his rifle. The next instant, we saw a puff of smoke from a bush, off to the left, and that sharp-shooter came plunging down, headforemost out of the tree, dead as Hector. Our man had crept round so that when the Federal slid around the tree, he exposed his body, and the Texan shot him.

Robert Stiles, the Adjutant of the Battalion, who had been, until lately, a member of our Battery, and was very devoted to it, and his comrades in it, had come to the lines to see how we were getting on, and gave us news of other parts of the line. He, Beau Barnes, and others of us were standing by our guns, talking, when a twenty pounder Parrott shell came grazing just over our guns, passed on, and about forty yards behind us struck a pine tree, about two and a half to three feet in diameter. The shell had turned. It struck that big tree sideways, and cut it entirely off, and threw it from the stump. It fell in an upright position, struck the ground, stood, for an instant, and then, came crashing down. It was a very creepy suggestion of what that shell might have done to one of us. A few moments after another struck the ground right by us and ricochetted. After it passed us, as was frequently the case, we caught sight of it, and followed its upward flight until it seemed to be going straight up to the sky. Stiles said "There it goes as though flung by the hand of a giant." Beau Barnes, who was *not* poetical, exclaimed, "Giant be darned; there ain't any giant can fling 'em like that." He was right!

Strange how the most trivial incidents keep their place in the memory, along with the great events, amidst which they occurred! I remember the fall of that tree, and the remark about that shell, and a small piece of pork which an Arkansas soldier gave me, and which, in jumping to the guns, I dropped into a mudhole, and never found again, though I fished for it diligently in the muddy water, and a *pig*, which was calmly rooting around near our guns, under fire, and which we watched, hoping he would be hit, so that we could get his meat, before the infantry did, to satisfy our wolfish hunger, just as distinctly as the several fierce battles which were fought that day.

About five o'clock the Federal guns on the hill in our front broke out again into a furious fire. It was a warning! We knew it meant that the infantry were about to charge again. We got to our guns, and the Texans stood to their arms. It seems that the balance of Hancock's Corps had got up, and now, with Warren's, and part of Sedgwick's Corps, formed in our front, Grant was going to make the supreme effort of the day, to break our line.

What we saw was that far down in the woods, heavy columns of men were moving; the woods seemed to be full of them. The pickets, and our guns opened on them at once. The next moment they appeared, three heavy lines one close behind the other. As they reached the edge of the woods, our lines were blazing with fire. But on they came! The first line was cut to pieces, only to have its place taken by the next, and then, the next. Closer and closer to our guns they pressed their bloody way, until they were within fifty yards of us. Heavens! how those men did strive, and strain to make their way against that tempest of bullets and canister! It was too much for man to do! They stopped and stayed there, and fired and shouted, under our withering fire. The carnage was fearful. Their men were being butchered! Their lines had all fallen into utter confusion. They could not come on! Despair suddenly seized them! The next moment a panic stricken cloud of fugitives was fast vanishing from our view, and the ground over which they had charged was blue with corpses, and red with blood.

From the Rapidan to Richmond and the Spottsylvania Campaign

Eggleston's Heroic Death

Just here, we of the "Howitzer" suffered our first, and only, loss in this day's fighting. Cary Eggleston, "No. 1" at third gun, had his arm shattered, and almost cut away from his body, by a fragment of shell. He quietly handed his rammer to John Ayres, who that instant came up to the gun, and said, "Here Johnny, you take it and go ahead!" Then, gripping his arm with his other hand, partly to stop the fast flowing blood, he turned to his comrades, and said in his jocular way, "Boys, I can never handle a sponge-staff any more. I reckon I'll have to go to teaching school." Then he stood a while, looking at the men working the gun. They urged him to go to the rear; he would not for a while. When he consented to go, they wanted to send a man with him, but he refused, and walked off by himself. As he passed back an infantry officer, seeing what an awful wound he had, and the streaming blood, insisted that one of the men should go and help him to the hospital. "No," he said; "I'm all right, and you haven't got any men to spare from here." So, holding his own arm, and compressing the artery with his thumb, he got to the hospital.

His arm was amputated, and a few days after, as the battery passed through Spottsylvania Court House, we went by the Court House building, used as a hospital, where he lay on the floor, and bade him "good-bye." He was just as cheerful, and bright, as ever, and full of eager interest in all that was going on. Said "Since he had time to think about it, he believed he *could* handle a sponge-staff *with one hand*; was going to practice it soon as he could get up, and would be back at his post *before long*." The next day, the brave young fellow died. The "Howitzers" will always remember him tenderly. No braver, cooler warrior ever lived! Always bright, full of fun in camp, and on the march, he was at the gun in action, the best "No. 1" I ever saw. One of the few men I ever knew who really seemed to enjoy a fight. His bearing, when he was wounded, was simply *heroic*. No wounded knight ever passed off his last battlefield in nobler sort. All honor to his memory!

John Ayres, the fellow to whom Cary Eggleston handed his rammer, was at his home in Buckingham County, Virginia, on furlough, when we started on the campaign. Off in the remote country, he didn't hear of our movements for several days. The moment he heard it, off he started, walked thirteen miles to the James River Canal boat; got to Richmond, came up to Louisa County on the Central Railroad, got off and walked twenty-three miles across country, guided by the sound of the battle, and reached his gun just in time to take Eggleston's place as "No. 1" and finish the fight.

When the enemy had thus broken in such utter rout, and with such fearful losses, we did hope they would let us alone, for this day at least. We were wet, and hungry, and nearly worn out working the gun, off and on all day, and it was late in the afternoon. For an hour or more things were quiet; the woods in front seemed deserted and still; the Texans were lying stretched out on the ground, all along the line; many of them asleep. We cannoneers were wearily sitting about the guns, wishing to gracious we had something to eat, and could go to bed, even if the *bed were* only one blanket, on the wet ground.

Our rifled guns had just been firing at a Federal battery which we could see, up on the hill in front of us. Watching the effect of the shots, we saw one of the caissons blown up, and a gun disabled, and soon confusion. Somebody remarked, "how easy it would be to take that battery, if any of our infantry were in reach." Just then, we heard loud cheering, which sounded to us, to be up in the woods, on our left, where Hill's men were. Someone instantly cried out, "There it goes now! Hill's men are going to take those guns." We eagerly gathered at the works, some distance to the left of our guns, where we could see better, and stood gazing up at the edge of the field, expecting every moment to see Hill's troops burst out of the woods, and rush upon these guns. Our attention was absorbed, off there, when, all of a sudden, one of our fellows who happened to glance the other way, yelled, "Good heavens! look out on the right." We all looked! There, pouring out of the woods, yelling like mad men, came the Federal infantry, fast as they could run, rushing straight upon our line. The whole field was blue with them! When we first saw them, the foremost were already within one hundred yards of our works, and aiming for a point about two hundred yards to our right. The breath was about knocked out of us by the suddenness of the surprise! It was not Hill's men charging *them*, but these fellows charging us,—whose yells we had heard, and here they were, right upon us! In two jumps we were at our gun. We had to turn it more to the right, and, with the first shot, blow away a light traverse, which was higher than the level of the gun, before we could bear on their columns. We sent two or three canisters tearing through their ranks; the Texans were blazing away, but, they had got too close to be stopped. The next instant, they surged over our works like a great blue wave, and were inside.

From the Rapidan to Richmond and the Spottsylvania Campaign

"Texas Will Never Forget Virginia"

So sudden was the surprise that they bayonetted two of the Texan infantry, asleep upon the ground. Soon as they got over they turned, and began to sweep down the works, on the inside, upon our guns. As the Texans forced to retire streamed past our guns, leaving us all alone and unsupported to face the enemy, Lieutenant Anderson said, "Men, the road is only a little way back of us; we must stay here, and stop these people, or the Army is cut in two. Run the guns back and open on them. We can hold them until help comes." We turned the guns round so as to command the approaching enemy, and chocked them with rails; several men snatched up the pile of ammunition, and piled it down before the guns in their new place, then we opened, with double canister.

If ever two guns were worked for all they were worth, those were! I don't believe any two guns, in the same time, ever fired as many shots as those two "Napoleons" did. We kept them just *spouting canister*! Several times *three canisters* were fired. Billy White, "No. 2," had only to reach down for them, and he would have loaded the guns *to the muzzle* if "No. 1" had given him time. The gun got so hot that, once, in jumping in to put in the friction primer, the back of my left hand touched it, and the skin was nearly taken off. The sponge was entirely worn off the rammer, so "No. 1" stopped sponging out the gun, and only rammed shot home. We fired so fast that the powder did not have time to ignite in the gun. After firing the gun, "No. 4" could hardly get the "primer" in before the gun was loaded, and ready to fire again. So it went on! It was fast and furious work! And the bullets sounded like bees buzzing above our heads.

I felt a sharp pain, then a numbness in my right hand. I glanced at it, and saw that the back of it was cut open, and bleeding. I had to pull the lanyard with my left hand the rest of the fight. I supposed a bullet had done it, but was disgusted to see blood on one of the rails, which chocked our gun, and find that this rail had worked loose, and, when struck by the recoiling gun wheel, had flown round and struck my hand, and disabled it. So, it was not an "honorable" wound, even though received in battle, as it was not done by a missile of the enemy.

Minute after minute, this hot work went on. The enemy, in coming over our works, and sweeping around, was thrown into disorder, so that they advanced on us in a confused mass.

In this mass our canister was doing deadly work, cutting lanes in every direction. Still on they came; getting slower in their advance as the canister constantly swept away the foremost men. The men in front began to flinch, they were within thirty yards of us,—firing wildly now. One good rush! and their bayonets would have silenced our guns! But they could not face that hail of death any longer; they could not make that rush! They began to give back from our muzzles.

At that moment, the Texans having rallied under the bank, forty yards to our right, and rear, came leaping like tigers upon their flank. The Texans were perfectly furious! It was the first time during the whole war that they had been forced from a position, under fire, and they were mad enough to eat those people up. A screaming yell burst out, a terrific outbreak of musketry, a rush, with the bayonets, and the inside of our work was clear of all, save the many dead, and wounded, and six hundred prisoners.

We ran our gun instantly back to its place, in the works, and got several shots into the flying mob, outside.

Then all was gone, and we were ready to drop in our tracks, with the exhausting work of the ten minutes that we had held the foe at bay.

General Gregg came up to our gun. With strong emotion he shook hands with each of us; he then took off his hat, and said, "Boys, Texas will never forget Virginia for this! Your heroic stand saved the line, and enabled my brigade to rally, and redeem its honor. It is the first time it ever left a position under fire, and it was only forced out, now, by surprise, and overwhelming weight. But it could not have rallied except for you. God bless you!" This moment Bob Stiles came up at a run. He had left the guns a few moments before the attack came, and hearing our guns so busy came back.

When General Gregg told him in a very enthusiastic way what we had done, he just rushed up to each cannoneer, and hugged him with a grip, strong enough to crush in his ribs, and vowed he was going to resign his Adjutancy at once, and come back to the guns.

Pretty soon Major-General Field, commanding part of the line, came dashing up on his horse, and leaped off. He went round shaking hands with us, and saying very civil things. He was red hot! He had witnessed the whole thing from his position, on a hill near by. He said, "When he saw the Federals roll over our works, and the Texans fall back, he was at his wits' end. He did not have a man to send us, and thought the line was hopelessly broken." Then he saw us turn our two guns down inside the works. He said to his courier, "It isn't possible these fellows will even attempt to keep their guns there. The enemy will be over them in two minutes." But as our guns roared, and the enemy slowed down, he swung his hat, as the courier told us, and yelled out, "By George, they will do it!" and clapping spurs into his horse he came tearing over to find the Texans in their line, all solid again. He said to us, "Men, it was perfectly magnificent, and I have to say that your splendid stand saved the Army from disaster. If the line had been broken here I don't know what we should have done."

Of course all this was very nice to hear. We tried to *look* as if we were *used to this sort of thing all the time*. But, it was something for us, young chaps, to have our hands shaken nearly off, by enthusiastic admirers, in the shape of Brigadier and Major-Generals, especially as they were such heroic old veterans as Field and Gregg, and to have the breath hugged out of us by an old comrade. All this glory was only to be divided up among *nine men*, so there was a big share for each one. I must confess, it was very pleasant indeed to hear that men, who were judges, thought we had done a fine thing; and when in General Orders next day our little performance was mentioned to the whole army in most complimentary terms, and we knew that the folks at home would hear it, I am free to say, that we would *not* have "taken a penny for our thoughts."

Contrast in Losses and the Reasons Therefore

The fight was over, just about as dusk was closing in. In this, and the fight at five o'clock, the enemy lost about six thousand men, killed and wounded. In the assaults, at *ten*, *eleven* and at *three* o'clock, they certainly lost between two and three thousand in killed and wounded, so this day's work cost them about seven or eight thousand in killed and wounded, besides prisoners.

Our loss was very small. On our immediate part of the line, almost nothing. In the battery, we had one man wounded at five o'clock. In this furious close up fight with infantry, with the awful mauling our guns gave them, strange to say, we had not a man touched. The only blood shed that day, at the "4th" gun, was caused by that rail striking my hand. And our battle line was just as it was, in the morning, save for the hecatomb of dead and dying in front of it, and six hundred prisoners we held inside.

From the Rapidan to Richmond and the Spottsylvania Campaign

About these prisoners: Numbers of these men were drunk, and officers too. One Colonel was so drunk that he did not know he was captured, or what had happened. The explanation of this fact, I do not profess to know, but *this* was what *the men themselves told us,* "That before they charged, heavy rations of whiskey were issued, and the men made to drink it. I know that indignant denial has been made of this charge, that the Federal soldiers were *made drunk* to send them in, but *this* I do *certainly know,* as an eye witness, and hundreds of our men know it too, that here, on the Spottsylvania line, and at Cold Harbor, and other times in this campaign, we captured numbers of the men, assaulting our lines, who were very drunk, and said they were made to drink. And this fact is one reason for the carnage among them, and the light loss they inflicted upon us. It made their men shoot wildly, and the moment our men saw this, they could, with the cooler aim, send death into their ranks. These hundreds of men going, *drunk,* to face death was a horrible sight; it is a horrible thought, but *it was a fact.*

Why Captain Hunter Failed to Rally His Men

In the quiet time, just before that sudden rush which swept over the works, Captain Hunter, of the Texans, was frying some pieces of fat bacon in a frying pan, over a little fire just by our gun. In a flash, the enemy was over the work, and we were in the thick of battle, and confusion. The Captain glanced from his frying bacon, to see his company falling back from the works, and the enemy pouring over. The sudden sight instantly drove him wild with excitement! He utterly forgot what he was doing. With a loud yell, he swung that frying pan round and round his head,—the hot grease flying in all directions,—and rushed to his men, and tried to rally them. (Having *lost the meat*, he *failed*! With a frying pan full of meat he could have rallied the regiment!) Back he fell with the brigade, and disappeared under the hill.

When the rallied Brigade came whooping back upon the enemy, ten minutes after, who should be in front tearing up the hill, leading the charge, but the gallant Captain, yelling like everything, and still waving that frying pan, to cheer on his men. More gallant charge was never led, with gleaming sword, than was this, led with that Texas frying pan.

At the time we were getting our guns around to fire upon the enemy inside the works, as the retiring Texans were falling back past us, Dr. Carter stepped quickly out, and in his courteous manner, called out to them, "Gentlemen, dear gentlemen, I hope that you are not running." A passing infantryman, a gaunt, unwashed, ragged chap, replied, "Never you mind, old fellow! We are just dropping back to get to 'em." "I beg your pardon," retorted the Doctor, "but if you want to *get to them*, you ought to *turn round*; they are not the way you are going." They passed on, and the fight took place. When it was over we noticed that the Doctor was very much vexed about something. We asked what was the matter? He said, "Never mind!" We insisted on his saying what disturbed him so. At last, he said "Well, I don't see why, because men are in the army, they should not observe the amenities customary among gentlemen." "Well," we said, "that is all right; but why do you say it?" "Why!" he warmly said; "did you hear that dirty, ragged infantryman call me an old fellow? A most disrespectful way to address a gentleman!"

All the row of the fight had not put it out of the Doctor's mind, and he brooded over it for some time. He never did get used to the lack of "amenities" and he always had an humble opinion of that unknown Texan, who did not observe the form of address customary among gentlemen. The Doctor himself always followed his own rule; he was as courteous in manner, and civil in speech, as "observant of the amenities" in the thick of a fight, as in his own parlor.

This was the first battle the Doctor was in, having lately joined us. As we ceased firing, one of us exclaimed, as we were apt to do, when a fight was over, "Well! that was a hot place." The Doctor turned on him and eagerly said, "Did I understand you to say that was a hot place?" "I did, indeed, and it was." The Doctor turned to another, and another, with the same eager question, "Did *you* think that was a hot place?" "Yes," we all agreed, "it was about as hot a one as we ever saw, or cared to see." "Well," said the Doctor, in a very relieved tone, "I am very glad to hear you gentlemen, who have had experience, say so. I hesitated a long time about coming into the army, because I did not want to disgrace my family, and I was afraid I should run, at the first fire; but, if you call *that* a hot place I think I can stand it." The Doctor's distrust of himself was very funny to us; for he was so utterly fearless, and reckless of danger, that some of the men thought, and said, that he tried to get himself shot. And once, the Captain threatened to put him under arrest, and send him to the rear, if he did not stop wantonly exposing his life. He had very little cause to distrust his courage, or fear that he would "disgrace his family" in *this*, or *any other way*.

From the Rapidan to Richmond and the Spottsylvania Campaign

When the fight was over, we promptly went among the Federal wounded, who lay thickly strewn on the inside of our lines, to see what we could do for their comfort and relief. Curious how one could, one minute, shoot a man down, and the next minute go and minister to him like a brother; so it was! The moment an enemy was wounded he ceased to be thought of as an enemy, and was just a suffering fellow man.

We did what we could for these wounded men, giving water to some; disposing the bodies of some in a more comfortable position, cheering them all up with the promise of prompt aid from the surgeons.

Among many others, we came to one man, mortally wounded and dying. His life was fast ebbing way; he was perfectly aware of his condition. He earnestly entreated that some one of us would pray for him. The request was passed on to Robert Stiles, who was still at our guns.

He came at once! Taking the hand of the poor dying fellow tenderly in his own, Stiles knelt right down by him on that wet, bloody ground, and, in a fervent prayer commended his soul to God. Then, as a brother might, stayed by him, saying what he could to comfort the troubled soul, and fix his thoughts upon the Saviour of men, and have him ready to meet his God.

Some of us looked reverently on with hearts full of sympathy in the scene. It was a sight I wish the men of both armies could have looked upon. Right on the bloody battlefield, surrounded by the dead and dying, that Confederate soldier kneeling over that dying Federal soldier praying for him.

Well! the long weary day of battle was closing and the fighting was done, at last. This 10th of May was a day filled up with fun, and fasting, and furious fighting; simple description, but *correct*. Thirteen to sixteen lines of infantry we had broken, and repulsed, during that day; and what between infantry and artillery we were under fire all day from five A. M. to nine o'clock that night; had toiled all night long, the night before; not a morsel had passed our lips all day, but one small crustless corn cake, taken out of a wet bag that had lain for hours, in the rain. A tired lot, we lay down that night on the wet ground to sleep, and be ready for the morrow. We fell asleep with the artillery still roaring on the lines, and shells still screaming about in the dark, and slept a sound dreamless sleep all through the night.

From the Rapidan to Richmond and the Spottsylvania Campaign

The next day, *the 11th*, was, for the most part, quiet and uneventful! The bloody and disastrous repulse of every effort of the enemy to force our line, had, as it well might, discouraged any further attempt along our front. From time to time we could hear the Federal artillery, on our front or other parts of the line, feeling our position, with an occasional reply from our guns.

The sharp-shooters of both sides were keeping up their own peculiar fun. At every point of vantage, on a hill, or behind a stump, or up a leafy tree, one of these marksmen was concealed, and would try his globe-sight rifle on any convenient mark, in the way of a man, which offered on the opposite line. Any fellow who exposed himself soon heard a bullet whistle past his ear, too close for comfort. Several of us had narrow escapes, but the only casualty we suffered was Cornelius Coyle. Coyle was from North Carolina and it seems that the jokes we were wont to indulge in at the expense of the "Tar Heels" had gotten him sore on the subject. In order to show us that a "Tar Heel" was as careless of danger as anybody else, he exposed himself, very unnecessarily, by standing on the works and on the guns, while the rest of us were "roosting low," and about two o'clock he got a bullet in the thigh, which disabled him, I believe, for the rest of the war. It was bad judgment! The jokes on the "Tar Heels" were only meant in fun. Nobody ever doubted the courage and gallantry of the North Carolinians. They had proved it too often, and were proving it every day! It did not need for Coyle to expose himself to prove it to us, and by his mistake we lost a good soldier.

The coming of night found all quiet on the lines. In the late afternoon, and early night, we could plainly hear the sound of,—what we took to be,—wagon trains and artillery, over in the enemy's lines, passing off to our right. We got therefrom the impression that the Federals were leaving our front and that by morning they would all be gone. So we were not surprised when a courier came with the orders from headquarters that we should get our guns out of the works, limber up, and be ready to move at daylight.

Having "A Cannon Handy"

We drew our gun from its place at the works, up the little incline we had made for its more easy running forward, hitched its trail to the pintle-hook of the limber, chocked the wheels, and left it there until we should move. The men picked out the least wet spots they could find, and lay down to sleep. Everybody was very tired, nearly worn out with the incessant work, and marching, and watching, and fighting, of the last seven or eight days and nights. This was the first really quiet night we had known for a week! The quiet and the assurance that the enemy was gone from our front, and that there was no need to bother about them, lulled the men into deep slumber. The infantry was all stretched out along the lines sleeping, and even the pickets out in front were, I am sure, sound asleep.

Every soul of our cannoneers was asleep, except Sergt. Dan. McCarthy, Beau Barnes, Jack Booker, and myself. We sat together, by the gun, talking and smoking until midnight. Then Jack said he would go to bed, and did. We three, McCarthy, Barnes and I, continued our conversation for some time longer, for no special reason, except perhaps, that we were too tired to move, and we sat there, in the dark, listening to the rumbling of heavy wheels over in the Federal lines, and talking about the events of the last few days, speculating about what was to come. Then our thoughts ran on other days, and scenes, and the folks at home, and we talked about these until we became quite sentimental.

Several times it was suggested that we had better go to sleep, but we talked ourselves wide awake. About two o'clock it was again suggested, but Dan said he did wish we had something to eat first. This was a most agreeable thought, and in discussing the same it was discovered that I had a corncake, Dan had some coffee, and Beau some sugar. So we resolved, before lying down, to go back under the hill, some fifty yards behind the works, where a fire was kept burning or smoldering all the time, and have a little supper of bread and coffee, which we proceeded to do. We made up the fire, got water from the branch, warmed our corncake, boiled the coffee, got out our tin cups, and sat around the fire having a fine time. It was now about time for daybreak, though still very dark. Dan proposed that we stroll up to the guns, and lie down awhile. We walked slowly up! When we got to the guns all was still, and quiet, as when we left, and I really believe we three were the only men awake on that part of the line.

Before lying down Dan and I stepped to where our gun had been, and stood a moment looking out through the dim light, which had hardly begun, of a dark cloudy morning.

We had no object in this outlook, it was the instinct of a soldier to look around him before going to sleep. It was, I think, the Providence of God to an important result. For most fortunate indeed was it that we took that glance out toward the front.

From the Rapidan to Richmond and the Spottsylvania Campaign

As our eye rested upon the edge of the wood out to our right front, we caught a vague glimpse of movement among the trees. We called Barnes, and stood together, watching keenly. Presently the air lightened a little, and we could discern the dim figures of men moving about, just within the woods. "Who are those men?" Dan asked. "Did either of you see any of the troops pass out of the lines during the night?" "No, we had not." "Then," he said, "I don't like this. Who can they be?" Just then the cloud seemed to lift a little, more light shot into the landscape, and, to our dismay, we clearly saw a line of men. Yes! no doubt now! That was a battle line of Federals, formed there in the edge of the woods, and just beginning to advance,—as silently as so many ghosts. There they were, two hundred yards off marching swiftly for our line, and everybody fast asleep in that line!

The horror of the situation flashed on us. The enemy would be bayonetting our sleeping, helpless comrades, and the line be taken in two minutes! What could we do to save them? Wake them up? No time to get a dozen men roused up before the fatal peril would be upon us. Suddenly! the same thought seemed to flash into our minds. Fire the gun! that will wake up the line instantly. Come boys! There was a case-shot in the gun. I remembered I had not fired it out, and I had my friction primer box on, and a primer hooked to the lanyard. We jerked the trail loose from the limber, and let the gun run to its place! Before it stopped, I think, I had the primer in, while Dan pulled the trail round to get the aim. He sprung aside as I let drive.

The crash of that Napoleon, and the scream of the shell there, in the deep stillness of day-dawn, sounded as if it might be heard all over Virginia! The effect was instant! You ought to have seen the boys, lying all about, "tumble up." They flirted up from the ground like snap bugs! "Gabriel's trumpet" couldn't have jerked them to their feet quicker.

Ned Barnes had lain down right where the gun had been, at the work. When we ran it back to its place, in our excitement, we did not notice him. Fortunately the wheels went on either side of him. He was lying flat on his back, and right under the gun, when it fired. Ned went on like a chicken with its head off. There was a scuffle, a yell, the whack of a bumped head under the gun. Ned came tumbling out, all in a heap, perfectly dazed, and wanting to know, in indignant tones, "What in the thunder we were doing that way *for*?"

From the Rapidan to Richmond and the Spottsylvania Campaign

Before the sound of our gun had died away the whole line was up, shooting like mad, and both guns were going hard. A few minutes of this sent that sneaking line back to the woods, with a good deal more noise, and faster, than it came. We learnt, afterwards, that the idea was to surprise us, if possible. If so, to take, and sweep our line. If not, *not* to press the attack. The "surprise" was all they could have wished. Not a picket fired on them. They were in one hundred and fifty yards of our sleeping men, and could have simply walked over them, and captured the whole line at that point. And, *if they had*— fixed as our Army was, a half hour later—it would, I am sure, have meant disaster. The only thing that averted it was, *humanly* speaking, the *accident* that three young "Howitzers" sat up talking all night, and, happened to look over at that wood at the break of day,—and *had a cannon handy*!

I think the Texans "owed us another one" for this, and the Army of Northern Virginia "owed us one" too. Major-General Field *said so* in his report of this incident.

The very same thing which *would have happened here was happening* five minutes later up the line to our right, where the Federal troops came right over our works, and caught our exhausted soldiers asleep in their blankets—the start of the bloody business of the Bloody Angle.

Yes! the bloody work which was to go on all day long, this dreadful 12th of May, was already beginning, up there in the woods.

The little firing on our part of the line was scarcely over, before we heard the sound of musketry come rolling down the line from the right. Soon the big guns joined in, and we knew that a furious fight was going on, off there. In a few moments we got the news, called from man to man down along the lines, "The Yankees have taken the Salient on Ewell's front, and captured Ed. Johnson's Division, and twenty guns. Pass it down the lines!"

So it was! In overwhelming masses the Federals had poured out of the woods, over the Salient Angle, where the men were asleep, and from which the cannon had been withdrawn. And General Lee was trying to drive them out, and retake our works.

This was the great business of the 12th of May. A very cyclone of battle raged round that Salient. The Federals trying to hold it, our men trying to retake it. We heard that the two Parrott guns of our "Right Section" had gone over there to help, and they were in the

From the Rapidan to Richmond and the Spottsylvania Campaign

thick of that awful row. We heard it all going on, artillery and musketry, rolling and crashing away, all day long.

Our part of the line was comparatively quiet, after the fight of the early morning. Several times infantry was seen moving about, down in the woods, in our front, and we would send a few shells into the woods just to let them know that we were watchful, and ready. Harry Sublett was wounded by a stray ball on this day. But no real attack was made, only the sound of the sharp-shooter's rifle, and the sound of their bullets enlivened the time.

This went on for several days. The idea of breaking our line, here, had been given up as a hopeless job, and no other attempt was made on it. Assaults were made on other points, and we could hear fighting, here and there, but we were left alone.

At last, we got orders to move, about the 18th or 19th. Our pickets had advanced through the woods, and reported that the enemy had left our front.

While waiting for the horses to be brought up to take off the guns, an infantryman told me that a cow had been killed, between the lines, and was lying down there in the woods, in front.

We had had an awful time about food, for the last week, and were hungry as wolves. This news about the cow was news indeed. I told several of the boys, and off we started to get some of that cow! We found it lying just in the edge of the woods. It was a hideous place to go for a beefsteak! All around, the ground was covered with dead Federal soldiers, many in an advanced stage of decay. The woods had been on fire, and many of these bodies were burned; some with the clothing, and nearly all the flesh consumed! The carcass of that cow was *touching five dead bodies,*—which will give an idea of how thick the dead were lying. Many of their wounded had perished in the flames, which had swept over the ground.

Grant's Neglect of Federal Wounded

We had witnessed all these horrors, with our own eyes, days before, from our lines, and had been helpless to do anything for them. Hundreds of wounded Federal soldiers lay between the lines, day after day, and perished for want of help. Several of us, unable to bear the sight of their suffering, went out one day to carry them food and water, and the Federals fired upon us, and wounded one of our men, then we had to leave them alone. They could not or would not care for their wounded, and would not let us do it. It *was stated* among us that General Lee had sent an offer to General Grant to permit him to send, and care for his wounded, near our lines; and he refused. And then General Lee offered, if Grant would suspend hostilities for some hours, that *we* would care for his wounded rather than see them suffer, and die, before our eyes; Grant refused that proposal too!

Certain it is, these poor fellows were left to their fate and perished, miserably, by wounds and famine, and fire. Their many dead, in our front, lay unburied until the odor from them was so dreadful that we could hardly stay in our works. It may be that General Grant had this in mind, and was determined that, if his *live* soldiers couldn't drive us out of the works, his *dead* ones should. Well! he had his way of making war! And on account of his inhumanity to his wounded, his *own men* thought as *ours did*, that his way was very brutal! I heard his own men curse him bitterly. They called him "The Butcher" in those days. The feeling of his army to him was widely different from our feeling for our General.

All those dead soldiers along a line of five miles lay rotting on the ground, until we had gone away, and the people of the country neighborhood had to collect them from the fields, and thickets, and bury them, for fear of pestilence. And when one remembers that from Thursday, the 5th of May, to Thursday, the 12th of May, General Grant had lost 40,000 in killed and wounded, the dread sight of death and suffering we looked upon, can be imagined! The thronging lines of unburied dead,—it was a shocking and appalling spectacle!

But we could not just then, mind the sights we saw! We got our beef, all the same! We were the first to get to that cow, and we had to take our knives and cut through the skin, on the rump, and flay it up, and then cut out hunks of the flesh, as best we could, and get back to the guns.

As I got back, carrying my big piece of meat, in my hands, Col. H. C. Cabell, commanding our Battalion, met me. He said, "My dear boy, where on earth did you get that meat?" I told him. "Well," he said, "I am almost starved; *could* you give me a little piece?" I cut off a chunk as big as my fist, stuck it on a sharp stick, held it a few minutes in a fire, close by, and handed it up to the Colonel, sitting on his horse. He took it off the stick, and ate it ravenously. He said it was the best morsel he ever tasted! It was scant times when a Colonel of artillery was as famished as he was! I cut up the rest of the beef, and divided among several of us, and we cooked it on a stick, the only cooking utensil we had at hand, and ate it, with a keenness of enjoyment that terrapin, canvass back duck, and Lynnhaven oysters could not provoke me to now. *My dear!* but that hot meat was good, to palates accustomed, mostly, to *nothing,* and *no salt on that,* for about a week. The only meat we had now,—when we had any at all.—was fat mess pork, and we ate that *raw.* Hot beef was a delicious change!

Meanwhile the hours had worn on. We limbered up the guns, and moved several miles off, toward the right, passing through Spottsylvania Court House. It was here we went by to see Cary Eggleston for the last time. He died next day.

We halted in a broom-sedge field, some distance beyond the Court House, and parked our guns, along with some other artillery, already there. And here we stayed a day or two.

The only thing I particularly recall of the stay here, was a trivial circumstance. One of the batteries we found in this field, belonged to the "Reserve Artillery" of which the "*un*reserved artillery" had a very humble opinion indeed,—just at that time.

These fellows had not fired a shot, through all the late fighting, and their guns were as bright, and clean as possible; which ours were not. One day a blue bird started to build her nest in the muzzle of one of their guns. Some of the sentimental fellows took this as an augury. "A sweet gentle little bird building her nest in the muzzle of a cannon! What *could* that mean but, that peace was about to be made, and these cannon useless?"

The rest of us scouted this fancy, and took it as a rare good joke on that "Reserve Artillery." We said "their guns were not of any use anyhow *except* for birds' nests; the birds knew they would be perfectly safe to build their nest, and live in *those* guns. *They* would not be disturbed!" We "chaffed" the officers and men of that battery most unmercifully. The whole field was on the *grin,* about that birds' nest. The poor fellows were blazing mad, and much mortified; so *disgusted* that they took their nice, clean guns, and went off to a distant part of the field, to get rid of us. We were *sorry* to lose them! They afforded *us* a great deal of fun, if they didn't have any themselves. That blue bird story got all over our part of the Army, and those "Reserve Artillerists" were "sorry that they were living."

CHAPTER IV

COLD HARBOR AND THE DEFENSE OF RICHMOND

About the 20th or 21st we started from Spottsylvania battlefields for others. The Army was on the move, and we went along. For a day or two we were constantly marching, not knowing where we were going, and along roads that I remember very little about. At last, about the 22d, we crossed the North Anna River, and struck the Central Railroad (now "the Chesapeake and Ohio") and marched along it, till we halted near Hanover Junction.

Our Army had crossed and stopped on the south bank of the North Anna, two or three miles in front of the Junction, and was taking the river for a new line of defence. Presently the Federal Army came up pushing on, for the same point, and found us, already ahead, in front, and across their track! Then they went at the same old game of trying to break through us. They got across the river on our right, and on our left. General Lee then threw back both wings of his army, clinging with his centre to the river bank. Thus check-mating Grant in a way to make his head swim! Grant after crossing the river, on both our right and left, suddenly found he had got his army cut in two, and he *got out of that*, just as quickly as he could, and gave the North Anna line up as a bad job.

We were moving in one direction, or another, about the Junction, for seven or eight days. This North Anna business was far more a matter of brains between the Generals, than brawn between the men. Some sharp fighting, on points right and left, but that was all! General Lee simply "horn swaggled" General Grant, and that was the end of it! We were out one day on the "Doswell Farm," and got under a pretty sharp infantry fire, and fired a few shots, then General Rodes' skirmishers charged, and drove them off, and we saw no more of them.

Along about the 29th or 30th of May, we got on the march again; this time through the "Slashes of Hanover." It was an all-night march, and a most uncomfortable one. The rain had been pouring, and long sections of the road were under water. I think we waded for miles, that dark night, through water from an inch to a foot deep. And the mud holes! after a time our gun wheels went up to the hub, and we had to turn to, there in the dark, and prize our guns out; nearly lift them bodily out of the mud. I suppose we did not go more than five or six miles, in that all-night march, and by the time day dawned we were as wet, and muddy, as the roads, and felt as *flat*, and were tired to death. We halted for an hour or two to rest; then pushed on, all day.

In the late afternoon (this I think was May 31st) we took our guns into position, on the far edge of a flat, open field. Two hundred yards in front of us, in the edge of a wood, was a white frame Church, which, some of the fellows, who knew this neighborhood, told us was "Pole Green Church." They also told us that the Pamunkey River was about a mile in front of us. We heard artillery in various directions, but saw no enemy, and did not know anything of what was going on, except where we were. It was quiet there; so we went to sleep, and were undisturbed during the night.

The next morning, we found that infantry had formed right and left of us, and we were in a line of battle stretching across this extensive field. About eleven o'clock skirmishers began to appear, in the woods, in front of us. They thickened up, and opened on us quite a lively fire. We stood this awhile until those skirmishers made a rush from the woods, and tried to gain the cover of the church building. Some of them did, and as this was crowding us a little too close, we took to our guns, and so dosed them with canister, as they ran out, that they retired, out of range, into the woods. Soon after some infantry began to form in the edge of the woods as if they were about to charge us. We opened on them. They advanced a little, then broke in some confusion, and disappeared. The rest of this day, June 1st, along where we were, there was lively sharp-shooting going on, up and down the line, and once a battery fired a few shots at us, but no special attack was made.

In the afternoon, taking advantage of the quiet, our negro mess cooks came into the line, to bring us something to eat. Each fellow had the cooked meat, and bread, for his mess, in a bag, swung over his shoulder. They came on across the field until within a hundred yards of the line, when a shell struck, in the field, not far from them. The darkies scattered, like a covey of birds! Some ran one way, and some another. Some ran back to the rear, and a few ran on to us. Our cook, Ephraim, came tearing on with long leaps, and tumbled over among us crying out, "De Lord have mercy upon us." "Ephraim," we said, "what is the matter? what did you run for?" All in a tremble, he thrust out the bag towards us, and exclaimed, "Here, Marse George, take your vituals, and let me git away from here. De

Lord forgive me for being such a fool as to come to sich a place as dis *anyhow*."

"But, Ephraim," we said, "there was no danger! That shell didn't hit anywhere near you." "De ain't no use in telling me dat! Don't nobody know whar dem things goin'! Sound to me like it was bout to hit me side my head, and bust my brains out, every minit; and if it had a hit me, dem other cooks would all a run away, and left me lying out dar, like a poor creeter." "But, my dear Ephraim," we said, "it mortifies us to see the 'Howitzer' cooks running so, with all the men looking on." "Don't keer who looking! When dem things come any whar bout me, I *bleeged* to run. Dis ain't no place for cooks, nohow. Here gentlemen! take your rations; I got to get away from here!" We emptied the bag, he threw it over his back, and streaked with it to the rear.

Another night in line here! Next morning, June 2d, orders came to move. We got on a road running along, just back of our position, and marched off toward the right. The road ran, for some distance, nearly parallel to our lines, and then bore away toward the rear. For a time we met, or passed bodies of troops and wagon teams on the roadside, soldiers single, or in groups. Further on, all these reminders of the presence of the Army were left behind, and we found ourselves marching on quiet lonely country roads, through woods and fields of a peaceful rural landscape. We had not the least idea where we were going; or what we were going to do, or see when we got there. But we had got out of the habit of caring for that.

The Last March of Our Howitzer Captain

It was a calm, sweet June evening! quiet country farms, and homes lay all about us. The whole scene spoke of peace. It was such a restful change to us from the din and smoke and crowd we had been in the midst of so long. We gave ourselves up to the influences of the hour, and a very pleasant evening we cannoneers had strolling along, in front of the column of guns, and talking together.

Captain McCarthy was on foot, in the midst of us, as we marched. I remember being particularly struck with what a stalwart, martial figure he was, as he strode along that road. He was much more silent, and quiet than usual! He was generally so bright and cheerful, that this was noticed, and remarked on by several of us.

It was afterwards, that perhaps a presentiment was given him that this was his last march, with the battery, he had fought so often, and loved so much; and *this* saddened, and softened his usually bold, soldierly spirit, and bearing. I walked and talked with him a good deal that afternoon, and certainly I was struck by a quietness of manner, and a gentleness of speech, not at all usual with him. But we did not know what it meant *then*! So we cheerily swung along that silent road, to meet what was coming to him, and to us, in the unseen way ahead.

About five o'clock we pulled out of the road we had been travelling, and followed a narrow farm road, across a wide, open field, toward a farmhouse, on its farther edge. Beyond the house was a large pine wood, which stopped all view in that direction. As we passed across that field, we saw some other artillery, coming from another direction, and converging with us upon that farmhouse. When we drew close together, we discovered that these fellows were the Second and Third Companies of the "Richmond Howitzers." Our Company, the First, had been separated from them at the beginning of the war, and they had never met, before now. A little while after, at this spot, the three batteries, "First," "Second" and "Third Richmond Howitzers" went into battle side by side, for the first, and *only* time, during the war. There was great interest felt by the boys that we should go into one fight *together*; but before we went in, the Battalion was broken up again, and scattered, to different parts of the line.

When we got near this farmhouse, all was quiet! We had not seen, or heard of any enemy for many hours, and we did not know where anybody was; didn't even know "where we were *at*" *ourselves*. The farm road ran past the house, round the barn and on toward that pine woods behind the house.

We halted just by the house, and got some water, at the well, and stood around and wondered what we were here for. There were some cherry trees, with ripe cherries on them, and up them the boys swarmed, Leigh Robinson gallantly leading the way, to enjoy the fruit.

We were thus engaged, when the deep quiet of this rural scene was suddenly, and rudely broken! Over beyond that wood just by us, there burst out a terrific roar of musketry! It was like a clap of thunder out of a clear sky! We did not know any troops were near us, and had no idea that the enemy was in ten miles of us.

From the Rapidan to Richmond and the Spottsylvania Campaign

But there right through those pines the musketry was rolling, and cracking now! A few cannon shots joined in, and the Confederate "yell" rose up out of the thunder of battle. And the bullets began to sing around us. The cherry trees were quickly deserted by all, but Leigh Robinson. He stayed up there with balls whizzing close to him, and calmly picked and ate cherries,—as if these were humming birds sporting about him,—until he had enough, or more likely, the cherries gave out. Not knowing who was fighting beyond the woods, or what might come of it, we got the guns into battery, facing the woods, to be ready for what might be.

In a few minutes we saw Colonel Goggin, of Kershaw's staff, dash out of the woods, and gallop toward us. He told us that it was Kershaw's Division over there. They had been attacked by heavy lines of the enemy; that our line was broken, and captured at one point, and that Kershaw wanted some guns, just as quick as they could get to him. Our two "Napoleons" were ordered in. Goggin said "for heaven's sake come at double quick;" the need was very urgent. We cannoneers of the Left Section had the guns limbered up, and into the woods, in about a minute; we, double-quicking alongside. We went by a narrow wood road, which entering the woods straight ahead of us, went obliquely to the left down a deep ravine, crossed a little stream, and up the hill, into the open field beyond.

Passing through that pine wood was a mean job! The Minie balls were slapping the pines all about us, with that venomous sound, with which a Minie crashes into green pine wood. It is a mean piece of work anyhow, to go from the rear up to a fighting line! But, away we went, excited and eager to get through, and see what was going on. The road, cut through the steep banks down to the stream, was so very narrow that it barely admitted our wheels, and when they went farther down the cut, our hubs stuck in the bank, on both sides, and the gun was held fast. From this point the road ran straight up to the edge of the wood. We could see men running about, and yelling, and shooting in the open ground. We could not tell whether they were our men or the enemy, and the fear seized us that the enemy might be pressing our people back, and would catch us, helpless and useless, in this ridiculous fix.

Gracious! how the driver did whip, and spur! and how the cannoneers did strain, and tug at those wheels! Captain McCarthy jumped off his horse, and put his powerful strength to the wheel. The men from the other guns joined us, and, at last, when we were

From the Rapidan to Richmond and the Spottsylvania Campaign

nearly wild with excitement, we gave one tremendous jerk, all together, and lifted the whole thing bodily out of that rut, and over the bank. The horses, as excited now, as we were, snatched the gun over the bank, across the stream, nearly upsetting it, and then went tearing, at a full gallop, up the hill; we running at top speed to keep up. The third gun following. At this pace, we dashed into the open field, and were upon the battle ground. We ran the guns into the line of battle, along a slight work Kershaw's men had hurriedly thrown up, just to the left of the part of the line which the Federals had taken, and were still holding. We pushed up, until we got an enfilade fire upon their lines. A few case-shots screaming down their line sent them flying out of that, and our line was restored.

The Colonel of one of their regiments, captured by our men, said that his regiment was lying down behind our captured line, and one of our shells cut down a large pine tree and threw it on his line, and about finished up what was left of his regiment. The shell burst just as it struck the tree, and the shell fragments, and falling tree together, killed twelve or fifteen men, and wounded a number of others.

The fighting was dying down now, and soon ceased. Our line restored, the enemy made no further effort to take it. The rest of the time, till dark, was taken up with sharp-shooting, and artillery fire. A farmhouse and outbuildings and barn stood right behind our position, and, I remember, the barn swallows in large numbers were skimming and twittering all around, through the sweet, bright air, while shells and balls were singing a very different sort of song. I never saw that sight during the war but this once,—birds flying about in the midst of a battle. But here, those dear little swallows circled round, and round that barn, and the adjoining field, for hours, while the air was full of flying missiles. They did not seem to mind it. Perhaps they wondered what on earth was going on. It was a curious scene!

During the night we made some little addition to the slight earth work, which the infantry had thrown up, in front of our two guns. Infantry began to pile into the line on both sides of our guns; we learned that this was the Twentieth South Carolina Regiment, Colonel Keitt, who had been killed, in a fight the Regiment had been in, that afternoon.

This regiment, at this time when some Brigades in the Army of Northern Virginia had not more than one thousand or twelve hundred men, came among us with seventeen hundred men ready for duty. The regiment had been stationed at Fort Sumter; had seen nothing of war except the siege of a Fort, and their idea of the chief duty of a soldier was,—to get as much earth between him and the enemy as possible. When they came into line this night, and saw this slight bank of dirt,—about two feet thick, and three feet high,—and learned that we expected, certainly, to fight behind it in the morning, they were perfectly aghast! They pitched in, and began to "throw dirt." They kept it up all night, and by morning had a wall of earth in front of them, in many places eight feet high, and six to seven feet thick.

How much higher, and thicker they would have got it, if the enemy had not interrupted them, gracious only knows! Of course they couldn't begin to shoot over it, except at *the sky*; perhaps they thought *anything blue* would do to shoot at and the sky was blue. But it was a fact, that when the enemy advanced next morning, this big regiment was positively "Hors du Combat."

It is true, that when we woke up at daylight, and found what they had done, we jeered, and laughed at them, and showed them the impossibility of fighting from behind that wall, until some of them got ashamed, and began to shovel down the top, a little. Captain McCarthy sent to let General Kershaw know the absurd situation we were in,—supported by infantry that could not fire a shot, and warning him, that if the enemy charged, they would certainly take the line, unless our two guns alone could hold it. General Kershaw sent orders to them "to shovel that thing down to a proper height," but they didn't have time to do it. When the fight began some of them had cut out a shelf on the inside of the bank, and some of them had gotten boxes and logs and a number stood up on them, and did some shooting, and behaved gallantly; but many of them seeming to think that a man should be "rewarded according to his works" laid closely down behind that wall, and never stirred.

The next night General Lee took them out of the lines, and gave them picks, and shovels, and made a "sapping and mining corps" of them,—the military service they were most fitted for, and they *were* rewarded according to their works.

While these beavers were gallantly wielding the pick and shovel, we, satisfied with our little bank of dirt, were getting ready for next day's work, by a good sound sleep. One of our boys did have misgiving about the strength of our defences. He went in the night, and woke

From the Rapidan to Richmond and the Spottsylvania Campaign

up Sergeant Moncure and said, "Monkey, don't you think these works are very thin?" "Yes, Tom, they are," he replied. "You just get a spade, and go and make them just as thick as you think they ought to be; Good night!" He resumed his slumbers, and Tom, not an overly energetic person, walked away grumbling that "the work *was* too thin, but he would be derned if *he* was going out there, in the dark to work on them, all by himself," which he didn't.

Somehow when we lay down this night we had gotten the impression that things were going to be rough, in the morning. They were!

Just as the day dawn was struggling through the clouds, we were roused by the sound of several guns, fired in quick succession. We were on our feet instantly, and saw that all was ready for action. Shells came howling at us from batteries that we could discern in the dim light. We could see the light of their burning fuses, as they started out of their guns, and could trace their flight toward us by that. Some of them would strike the ground in front, and ricochet over us; some would crash into our work, with a terrific *thud*, and some went screaming over our heads,—very close, too, and went on to the rear to look after our Right Section guns, which were still by that farmhouse, where we had left them, the evening before. They knocked down several of the shelter tents our boys were sleeping under, and several of our fellows, there, had the narrowest kind of an escape. One shell "caromed" over three of the men, who were sleeping side by side, touching the very blanket that was over them. The Right Section boys needed no reveille that morning to get them out! They tumbled up with great promptness and moved round out of the line of fire. Fortunately none of them were actually hurt, just here. One fellow was sleeping with several canteens of water hanging right over his head. A bullet went through them. He was nearly drowned!

The Bloodiest Fifteen Minutes of the War

In our front, this artillery fire kept up for a while, then it stopped! The next moment, there was an awful rush! From every quarter their infantry came pouring on over the fields, and through the woods, yelling and firing, and coming at a run. Their columns seemed unending! Enough people to sweep our thin lines from the face of the earth! Up and down our battle line, the fierce musketry broke out. To right and left it ran, crashing and rolling like the sound of a heavy hail on a tin roof, magnified a thousand times, with the cannon pealing out in the midst of it like claps of thunder. Our line, far as the eye could reach, was ablaze with fire; and into that furious storm of death, the blue columns were swiftly urging their way.

Straight in our front one mass was advancing on us and we were hurling case-shot through their ranks,—when, suddenly! glancing to the right, we saw another column, which had rushed out of the woods on our right front, by the flank, almost upon us, not forty-five yards outside our line. Instantly we turned our guns upon them with double canister! Two or three shots doubled up the head of that column. It resolved itself into a formless crowd, that still stood stubbornly there, but could not get one step farther. And then, for three or four minutes, at short pistol range, the infantry and our Napoleon guns tore them to pieces. It was deadly, and bloody work! They were a helpless mob, now; a swarming multitude of confused men! They were falling by scores, hundreds! The mass was simply melting away under the fury of our fire. Then, they broke in panic, and headlong rout!

Many fearing to retreat under that deadly fire, dropped down behind the stumps near our line, and when the others had gone, we ordered them to come in. Several hundred prisoners were captured in this way. To show what our works were,—I saw one tall fellow jump up from behind a stump, run to our work, and with "a hop, skip, and a jump," he leaped entirely over it, and landed inside our line. And a foolish looking fellow he was, when he picked himself up!

Just as the enemy broke, Ben Lambert, "No. 1" at "4th" gun, was severely wounded, in the right arm, just as he raised it to swab his gun. One of the boys took his place, and the fire kept on.

The great assault was over and had failed! Only ten or fifteen minutes was its fury raging! In that ten minutes, thirteen thousand Federal soldiers lay stricken, with death, or wounds. In those few moments, Grant lost nearly as many men as the whole British Army lost in the entire battle of Waterloo.

Just to our right the enemy got over our works, and the guns right and left of the break were turned on them. We heard a "yell" behind us, and round a piece of pines came Eppa Hunton's Brigade of Virginians, at a run; General Eppa on horse-back leading them in, at a gallop. The Virginians delivered their volley at the Federals inside

From the Rapidan to Richmond and the Spottsylvania Campaign

our lines, then sprang on them like tigers. Next minute the few, left of them, were flying back over the works.

In the thick of the fight, Barksdale's Mississippi Brigade, now commanded by General Humphreys, to which our Battery had been attached, being unengaged just at that time, heard that the infantry supporting us was not effective, and that the "Howitzers" were in danger of being run over. They requested permission to come to our help, and two Regiments came tearing down the lines to our position, manned the line by us, and went to work. What work these splendid fellows could do in a fight! We had been very uneasy about our supports, and were delighted to see the Mississippians, especially, as they had voluntarily come to our help, in such a handsome manner.

The spectacle in front of our line was simply *sickening*! The horrible heaps of dead lay so ghastly, and the wounded were so thickly strewn all over the field. To right, and to left, out in front, along our line, as far as we could see, this dreadful array of the dead and wounded stretched! It was pitiful to see the wounded writhing, and to hear their cries of agony. And here *again*, as at Spottsylvania, these wounded were left between the lines, to perish miserably, of hunger and thirst, and mortifying wounds.

Federal Troops Refuse to Be Slaughtered

When, a few days after, Grant sent to look after them they were nearly all dead. What they must have suffered before death came! But none of their own people seemed to care, and no effort was made to help them,—when they might have been saved. I wonder who will have to answer for the *unnecessary waste of life* and suffering in the "Army of the Potomac?" For the untold agony and death that *need never have been*! It was awful! We used to think it was *brutal*! And the *Federal soldiers* thought so too!

Some hours after this assault we saw the enemy massing for another. Their columns advanced a little way, and then stopped. We could see there was some "hitch," and sent a few shells over there, just to encourage any little reluctance they might have about coming on. These lines stood still, and came no further.

We learned, afterwards, that perfectly demoralized, and disheartened by the bloody repulse of the morning, the Federal troops, when ordered by General Grant to storm our line again, *mutinied in line of battle*, and *in the face of the enemy and refused to go*

From the Rapidan to Richmond and the Spottsylvania Campaign

forward. I witnessed that performance, but did not understand at the time, just what was going on. The grave meaning of it was, that the enemy's soldiers had distinctly quailed before our lines and declared their utter inability to take them. And *this* was the verdict—at the end—of General Grant's Army upon General Grant's campaign! Their heads were more level than their General's. They were tired of being slaughtered for nothing!

The moment the morning assault was over, the Federal artillery opened furiously, all along the line, and all day long, we were under a constant fire of cannon, and sharp-shooters.

Fifty yards behind our guns was a farmhouse, outbuildings, and yard full of trees. Shells aimed at us, rained into those premises all day. The house was riddled like a sieve, the trees were cut down, and the outbuildings, barn, stables, sheds, etc., were reduced to a heap of kindling wood.

A pig was in a pen, in the yard! Everything else on the place had been hit, and we watched with interest the fate of that pig. He escaped all day! Just after dark, a shell skimmed just over our gun, went screaming back into that yard, burst,—and—we heard the pig squeal. Some of the men, at once, started for the yard, and came back with the pig. Said "he was mortally wounded, and they were going to carry him to the hospital." I fear he did not survive to get there! We disposed of his remains in the usual way.

About noon we heard that our Right Section had been ordered into position, on the lines, some distance to our right, and that John Moseley, No. 8 at 1st gun, while with his caisson, back of the lines, had been killed. A stray bullet had pierced his brain. No one was with him at the time. He was found dead, in the woods.

Dr. Carter "Apologizes for Getting Shot"

The sharp-shooters swept all the ground about us, making it dangerous for any man to expose himself an instant. Dr. Carter took some canteens, and his cup, and went round under the hill behind us, to bring some water. With filled canteens, and tin cup, filled to the brim, carried in his right hand, he recklessly came back across the field, in rear of the line. Just before he got to us, a bullet struck his right thumb, and shattered it. He did not drop the cup or spill the water! He came right on, as if nothing had happened, offered us a drink of water out of the cup, and then courteously apologized to the captain for getting shot; who accepted his apology, and sent him off

From the Rapidan to Richmond and the Spottsylvania Campaign

to the hospital, to have his thumb amputated; which he did, and was back at his post, the first moment his wound permitted. When we condoled with him for the loss of his thumb, he said "*He* didn't care anything about the *thumb*; he could *roll cigarettes just as well with the stump*, as he ever could with the whole thumb. That seemed about all the use he had for his thumb,—to roll cigarettes. He was an artist at that!

In the afternoon three or four of us were standing in a group talking when one of the numberless shells that were howling by all day long, burst in our very faces. I distinctly felt the heat of the explosion on my skin, and grains of powder out of the bursting shell struck our faces, and drew blood. The concussion was terrific! It was a pretty "close call" to all three of us!

The stream of shells fired at our guns gradually cut away the top of our work, until it was so low that it did not sufficiently protect our gun. We feared that some of the shells would strike our gun, and disable it. To avert this, for many hours that day, from time to time, we had to take turns, and, with shovels, throw sand from the inside on the top of the work. In this way we managed to keep our defences up, but it was weary work, and we grew very tired. Still, there was nothing for it, but to keep on, and *we kept* on!

Death of Captain McCarthy

About six o'clock, there fell the saddest loss, to the battery, that it had yet been called to bear. Captain McCarthy stood up at the work to watch what was going on in front. One moment, I saw him, standing there;—the next instant, I heard a sharp crash, the familiar sound of a bullet striking, and McCarthy was lying, flat on his back, and motionless. We jumped to his side! Nothing to be done! A long bullet from a "globe sight" rifle had struck him, two inches over his right eye, and crashed straight through his brain. He lay without motion two or three minutes, then his chest rose, and fell, gently, once or twice, and he was still, in death.

And there, on that red field of war, with shells, and bullets whistling all about, over his dead face, dropped the tears of brave men, who loved him well, and had fought with and followed him long! We had seen his superb courage in battle; his patient bearing of hardship, his unfaltering devotion to duty always; his kind, cordial comradeship! We knew him to be a soldier, every inch, and a patriot to his heart's core!

From the Rapidan to Richmond and the Spottsylvania Campaign

We knew, and said, that among all her sons, Virginia had no braver son, than this one, who had died for her. Sadly we lamented—"What shall we do, in battle, and in camp, and on march, his form and face missing from among us?" There was not a sadder group of hearts along that blood-drenched line that evening, than ours, who bowed deeply sorrowing over the form of our dead captain. We took his body in our arms, and bore it to where we could place it in an ambulance.

It was sent to his home, and family, in Richmond, and buried in "Shockoe Cemetery." And now,—after thirty-two years have passed, we, the old "Howitzers," still carry the name of "Ned McCarthy" in our hearts! We keep his memory green; we think of him, and rank him as a typical Confederate Soldier. One who by his splendid courage and devotion shed luster upon the name.

His stalwart form has gone to dust. The light of his bright, brave face has long gone from our eyes; the soul-stirring war time—when we were with him—has long passed away. The changes and chances of this mortal life have brought many experiences to us who survived him. Our feet have wandered far, into many paths. We have toiled, and thought, and suffered, and enjoyed much, in the long years, since we last looked upon his form dead on the red field of "Cold Harbor." "The strong hours have conquered us" in many things. But—the noble memory of this man! as a patriot and a hero!

Ah! that lives in our hearts! The hearts of his comrades who, with their own eyes, saw him live and bear, and fight and die—for *Virginia*—and the South.

The battle of Cold Harbor ended Grant's direct advance on Richmond. He drew off in confessed defeat and inability to go on— afterwards, he advanced by way of Petersburg.

The operations on that line resolved themselves into a siege. That siege lasted through the fall and winter and early spring of '65, with many attempts to break our lines, which always failed.

On the second day of April, 1865, according to General Lee's own statement to General Meade, just after the surrender, the Army of Northern Virginia stood, with 27,000 men, holding a line thirty-two miles long; facing an army of 150,000 men. On that day our line was broken, and the retreat began.

From the Rapidan to Richmond and the Spottsylvania Campaign

Under the circumstances, the disentanglement of our army from that long line, and getting it on the march, with the enemy's powerful army close in their front, was a supreme display of, at once, the consummate generalship of General Lee, and the unshakable morale of the Southern troops.

The retreat continued for one week; we started from Petersburg Sunday, April 2, and reached Appomattox, Saturday, April 8th. On that day, after the hunger, exhaustion, and losses in the many fights along the way, the Army stood at Appomattox, ninety miles from Petersburg, with 8,000 men with arms in their hands; and they were as "game" as ever. On that morning of April 9th, when General Gordon surrendered his little force of 1,300 men, he had to surrender 1,700 Federal soldiers, and fourteen pieces of artillery, which he had just captured from the enemy, while driving back their encircling line more than a mile.

Then General Lee, unwilling for useless sacrifice, surrendered the army, because it was "compelled to yield to overwhelming numbers and resources"—and that Army of Northern Virginia, when it was surrendered, had behind it this remarkable, and proud record, that, in the many battles it fought during the war, it was never once driven from the field of battle; and it was as defiant, and ready to fight at Appomattox as it was at Manassas, the first battle four years before.

As we turn from that closing scene, let us take a parting glance at the facts which, duly considered, enable us to form a true estimate of the fight the South made in that struggle of the Civil War.

The history of that war may be briefly, but accurately comprehended in this short statement. During the four years, '61 to '65, the North put into the field two million, eight hundred thousand (2,800,000) men. They were well armed, well equipped, and well fed—also, it had a Navy.

During those four years, the South put into the field less than six hundred thousand (600,000) men. They were poorly armed, poorly equipped, and poorly fed—much of the time, very poorly indeed! And it had no Navy.

It took those 2,800,000 men, with the Navy, four years to overcome those 600,000 men. In doing so they lost the lives of one million (1,000,000) men—nearly double the whole number of men the South put into the field.

From the Rapidan to Richmond and the Spottsylvania Campaign

What these facts mean, the world will judge—the world has judged!
And the world has off its hat to the race who made that heroic fight!

Lightning Source UK Ltd.
Milton Keynes UK
UKHW010634140621
385483UK00001B/71